ATTACK THE CASINO'S VULNERABLE GAMES

•GAMES•

YOUR BEST BETS USING THE BEST
STRATEGIES AT THE BEST GAMES!

JOHN GOLLEHON

About The Author

John Gollehon is considered more than just an expert player; he is a trusted authority, having written extensively on all the games included in this book. Gollehon is recognized by the national media as an expert on casino gambling and is frequently cited in newspaper stories on gaming. He has also appeared on numerous television documentaries. Gollehon's writings span five decades, having first published a gaming newsletter in 1979. He is the author of 28 titles on beating the casino, many of them best-sellers.

In his books, Gollehon shows players the skills they need to build confidence and become a top player, teaching them the secrets of developing timing—when to lay back, and when to deliver that knock-out punch.

Cardoza Books by John Gollehon

Conquering Casino Craps
Commando Craps & Blackjack!
Casino Games
What Casinos Don't Want You to Know
Attack the Casino's Vulnerable Games

ATTACK THE CASINO'S VULNERABLE GAMES

·GAMES·

YOUR BEST BETS USING THE BEST STRATEGIES AT THE BEST GAMES!

JOHN GOLLEHON

CARDOZA PUBLISHING

Cardoza Books by John Gollehon
Conquering Casino Craps
Commando Craps & Blackjack!
Casino Games
What Casinos Don't Want You to Know
Attack the Casino's Vulnerable Games

To Gamblers Who Mean Business

Your decision to gamble is a personal one. It should take into account many things, not the least of which is your ability to wisely manage money. If you frequently overdraw your checking account, exceed your credit-card limits, or otherwise spend your money recklessly—buying on impulse, for example—suffice to say gambling is a bad idea. If you do decide to try your luck, promise yourself that you will stay within your means. Gambling can be fun. Don't let serious losses take your fun away.

Cardoza Publishing is the foremost gaming and gambling publisher in the world with a library of more than 200 up-to-date and easy-to-read books and strategies. These authoritative works are written by the top experts in their fields and with more than 10,000,000 books in print, represent the best-selling and most popular gaming books anywhere.

NEW REVISED EDITION!
Copyright © 2006, 2012 by John Gollehon
-All Rights Reserved-

Library of Congress Catalog Card No: 2011945697
ISBN 13: 978-1-5804-2304-5   ISBN 10: 1-5804-2304-3

Visit our website or write for a full list of Cardoza Publishing books

CARDOZA PUBLISHING
P.O. Box 98115, Las Vegas, NV 89193
Phone (800)577-WINS
email: cardozabooks@aol.com
www.cardozabooks.com

T TABLE OF CONTENTS

3. ATTACKING THE CASINO AT CRAPS   47

4. POWER PROGRESSIVE STRATEGY   77

INTRODUCTION

Listen to me closely—I want you to win! And I want to help you win, okay? Seriously, there are few things I enjoy more than seeing players walk away from a table with chips falling out of their pockets. I like winners. I like to play with winners. I immerse myself in a winning frame of mind every minute I'm in action.

You can call it positive thinking, confidence, whatever you want. There are probably a thousand ways to say it, but there is only one way to pull it off—to win and to win again!

If you've read any of my other books, you know how I feel about the "conditioning" of a player. Casinos have lots of ways of conditioning you—to lose, of course. But we can counter that effort, and we will as we progress through this book. You'll learn how to play the casino's most vulnerable games—the games that smart bettors play—and how to make the right bets and the right moves. Frankly, any good gaming author can teach you how to play, but I like to go one step further: I want to teach you how to win. What a difference it can make when you have the confidence to attack the casino!

Incidentally, I chose the strong verb *attack* in the book's title for a reason. Other verbs could have worked—*beat* the casino, *defeat* the casino, and so on, but I like *attack*! I like it because it suggests the winning frame of mind you should have the next time you're in the trenches slugging it out against the casino.

1 **BREAKING THE CASINO'S CODE**

THE THREE "BE'S" OF A WINNING ATTITUDE

1. BE ALERT

Be alert to what, you ask? Be alert to changing trends. Good players can spot opportunities. Streaks of wins, dealer busts, players flush with chips, even a generally favorable climate to play in. Sometimes that's all you need. But you must search it out. Don't just plop yourself down and start playing. After all, you are on a "search and attack" mission when you first play and every time you reboot a new session.

A key part of the casino's code is to encourage you to play. That's right, for longer than you probably intended, and perhaps at betting minimums that are higher than you wanted. They employ the most effective marketing tools imaginable to keep you at the tables or the machines. Break that code by limiting your play to only those times when you're winning. If you're not winning, take a break. As you'll learn in a later chapter, a couple of bad pops in a row and I walk. If a casino beats me with a one-two punch, it won't get a third shot. It's Break City for me as I regroup and plan my next session.

2. BE SERIOUS

I recall watching a group of young players in their early twenties laughing it up pretty well as they exited a blackjack table. I figured they had all won soundly, but as I overheard their conversation, I found out that wasn't the case at all. They had all been beaten soundly. And, apparently, it was funny.

If you can explain to me what's funny about losing, I'm listening. You take it in stride, sure, but you should feel it in the pit of your stomach just as I do. The only way to counter the effects of a loss is with a win. If you take anything from this chapter, take this truth: Wins counter losses.

You can't laugh them away any more than you can laugh those lost hundreds back into your wallet. Get serious. None of this has anything to do with your betting level. Big bettor, small bettor, makes no difference. If you're not serious about winning, I assure you, you won't.

You see, the entire ambiance of a casino is designed to put you in a fun mood, relaxed and off guard. The casino wants you to think that you're there to have fun, laugh it up, let loose, and forget what you're really there for. Don't become a victim of its clever code. If you're not in the casino to win money—serious money—you have no business being there in the first place. Why blow your hard-earned paycheck on what really isn't fun anyhow? Gambling, my friend, has two components: winning and losing.

Guess which one is the real fun?

3. BE SMART

I watched this same bunch of players wander over to the keno lounge as they counted what little money they had left. They were not only running out of money, they were running out of clues. What should they be doing? What shouldn't they do? They obviously played the game with no knowledge of percentages, or they wouldn't have played at all. Plainly said, keno is an expensive proposition. Sure, some dweeb will come along and hit 8 out of 8 spots for $50,000 and think he's the smartest gambler in town. Smart? Hardly. Lucky? You bet.

I can only hope that such a lucky player has the smarts to take it home and stuff it away in a bank fund, investment account, stocks, bonds, something—anything except taking another shot at the casino, because the casino will get it back. *All* of it! Why? Because chief among the casino's code are its percentages. Casinos rely on their percentages (their "PC") to keep them in the game 24/7. Know why casino managers sleep so well at night? Because they know they have the percentages on their side. They also know that players who knock down high-percentage wins almost always come back for more. And they get what's coming to them—they lose it ten times faster than they won it. And they're no longer laughing.

On the other hand, smart players are very familiar with percentages, and they fight the lowest ones they can find. In some cases, they don't have to fight because they've found percentages that might actually tip to their favor. Or they might find a game that has no percentages at all—that's right, there are games where you have only the skill of other players to contend with. It has always surprised me that so many players know so little about the different bets scattered among the casino games and the varying percentages offered. When you're shopping for a car, are you looking for a good deal or a bad deal? Why is "shopping" in a casino any different? Think about it.

A CRASH COURSE IN PERCENTAGES

I'm not going to overly complicate this for you. Here's all you really need to know about casino games that are based on house percentages: If the casino pays off your winning wager at something less than the true odds—that is, the likelihood of winning that bet—it has acquired an advantage over you. The actual percentage it keeps depends on how much or how little it underpays you.

In the chapter on craps, we'll talk more about this subject because craps is a game with lots of bets and lots of different percentages. But for now, let's list all the games, not just the smart ones, and their corresponding percentages. You'll quickly see which games and which bets are the good deals and which ones are the bad deals.

GAME	PERCENTAGE

BACCARAT　　　　　　　　　　　　　　　　　1.13%
Percentage is averaged over number of player-hands (1.24%) and banker-hands (1.06%) played, based on casino studies. Banker-hand is inclusive of commissions. Clearly, the banker-hand is the wiser choice. Does not reflect tie bets (14%).

BLACKJACK　　　　　　　　　　　　　　0.2% to 0.5%
Variations in game rules prevent listing specific percentages. Always shop for the best playing conditions: blackjack pays 3 to 2, dealer must stand on all 17s, double down on any two cards, double after split, re-split aces. Multiple decks increase percentage. Perfect basic strategy assumed. Professional-level card counting can produce an infrequent player advantage.

CARIBBEAN STUD POKER　　　　　　　　　　　　5.23%
Progressive jackpot bets increase percentage.

CRAPS　　　　　　　　　　　　　　0.2% to 16.67%
This game has the widest spread of percentages among 25 different bets. The best bet is the odds-bet taken when a point number is established on the pass-line or come. Singularly, the bet is fair, no house advantage, but it can only be made with a pass-line or come bet. Single odds effectively lowers the 1.41%

house advantage for the pass-line or come bet to 0.83%. Double odds games reduce it further to 0.61%. Triple odds, five-times odds, and ten-times odds (0.2%) are the better multiple odds offered by some casinos.

KENO   25% to 60%
New variations in this game have produced bets with percentages over 60%! Typical percentages vary from 25% to 35%, steep by any standards. The game offers big jackpots for modest bets, but virtually all low-risk, high-reward bets offered by casinos are costly in percentage terms.

LET IT RIDE   3.52%
This game has always struck me as more difficult to beat than the percentage would indicate. Tread lightly.

3-CARD POKER   2.33% to 7.25%
The same caveat applies. Of all the newer poker-based games, this one has attracted more players, especially those who like to play a system. Many players push up the percentages.

PAI GOW   3.0%
Popular among Asians.

REEL-TYPE SLOTS   2% to 20% and up
In general terms, the higher the coin denomination, the lower the percentage. Accordingly, players expect the lowest percentages on "high roller" slots. But do they get them? Who knows? In fact, all machines hide their percentages within the computer circuitry.

ROULETTE   1.35% to 5.26%
Don't let the low 1.35% fool you. You'll only find it in few casinos (mostly European) offering "surrender" or "en prison" on even-money wagers on "single zero" wheels. The great majority of wheels in the United States are "double zero" meaning there are 38 compartments where the ball might land: 18 red numbers, 18 black numbers, and 2 green numbers. Since

payoffs are based on 36 numbers, the 2 green numbers create the house advantage of 5.26% (1/19).

VIDEO POKER   0.6% to 8.5%

Video poker machines are the only "slot" machines that reveal their percentages based on the paytable, primarily the payouts for a full house and a flush in games with no wild cards. The best jacks-or-better machines pay out 9 coins for a full house and 6 coins for a flush (9-6) with a pair of jacks or better returning your bet. However, the most commonly found machines pay only 8-5 or worse.

THE PLAYER'S CODE

Before we start discussing all the vulnerable games to attack, we need to look in the mirror for a moment. My mention earlier of those incompetent players certainly was not indicative of the way you play, right? Of course not! But there are faults that even the most seasoned players have and don't realize it. The casinos don't even need to factor them into their winning code. They have enough going for them already; this is no time for largess.

Other gaming writers will argue with my notion that a good player can exercise some control (both good and bad) over the effects of percentages. Here's how I see it. To the extent that game percentages contribute to the outcome (a winning or a losing session), so can another kind of control—self-control. There are times when I believe that your own control is more important than the influence of percentages, especially in the short term and especially when the percentages are quite small. You should know that even small percentages can bite you in the long term, but let's talk short term for a moment. In the short term, you can almost throw out the percentages because just about anything can happen, including good things—many good things—unless you screw them up.

Case in point: My buddy, Phil, had just returned from a small tribal casino in Northern Michigan, and I was expecting his call to tell me how he did. But Phil never called. Somewhat worried about him (he's not the healthiest gambler on the planet), I called his home and his wife answered the phone. Turns out that she was up there with him and since Phil was resting from a rough trip, Nancy was anxious to fill me in. From the sound of her voice, I could tell it didn't go well.

Phil is a craps player, like I am. We used to make a great team. We both played easy at first and got aggressive when the table heated up. Yeah, I know, basic stuff. But Phil changed the rules—he'd go crazy on me—so I stopped playing with him. Anyhow, here's how the conversation went down:

"John, you know Phil, he wanted to play craps so badly and they only had one table open. And what's worse, there were no players! It drove him nuts. He never wants to play at a dice table by himself. You don't either, right?"

"Nope."

"So, all the way up there, a dice crew ready to go, and no players."

"Got it, Nancy."

"Well, I talked Phil into playing video poker with me. Within minutes, he hits a straight flush. Boy, did he get excited!"

"Good, but I know Phil. I can't imagine him sitting at a poker machine. He hates slots, you know."

"Oh yeah. Anyhow, another half-hour or so of pushin' buttons and bang! He hit the big one!"

"A royal flush? Is that what you're telling me?"

"Yep. The biggie. And he was on top of the world!"

"I would imagine. I've gotta razz him about that when I see him."

"No, don't!"

"Why not?"

"Well, he got paid for the royal in hundreds, ten $100 bills, plus he had some winnings left from his earlier hits. And he says to me, 'Nancy, I'm gonna go over and see if they've got any dice players yet.'"

"Uh-oh!"

"You're right. I wanted to head home, but he wanted to make one last walk past the tables. Nothing had changed. No players. So he says to the crew, 'Gimme the dice. I'll start the game for you. I've got a little ammo here I didn't expect.'"

"Hmm."

"John, I'm so mad at him. He left every last dollar on that dice table—all of his winnings!"

"Well, like I said, I know Phil. He wanted to play craps. Loves to play craps. Obviously, winning wasn't his objective. He had already accomplished that."

"It ruined our trip, John. This all happened on the day we were leaving for home."

"Yep, I understand."

"So, any advice, Mr. Expert?"

"Well, I know a good divorce attorney."

"Seriously."

"Tell him he has to change his focus. He has to focus on winning, not playing. But I've already told him that a thousand times. Holding on to a win has always been a problem for him. Even if his big win had come at the craps table instead, he still might have given it back."

Like I said, dear readers, I know Phil. And I don't think Phil is going to change. I don't like to end a chapter on a downer note, but I've included this story because I believe it might help some of you. Discipline, my friends, discipline with a capital "D." Of all the strategies you are about to learn, none is more important than self-control. I'll work on Phil—you work on yourself!

2 ATTACKING THE CASINO AT BLACKJACK

At one time the casino's signature game, blackjack has gone through considerable changes over the years. Casino bosses, even today, can't seem to keep their hands out of the toolbox. Someone has to tell them that the wagon ain't broke, so stop trying to fix it! It's important that you understand the game as it's played today, and not be misled by the attraction of the game's earlier features, which have gone the way of the 99-cent breakfast! Okay, maybe you can still find a cheap breakfast somewhere, but if you want to play "pure" blackjack, you'll need a time machine set for the 1960s. (Yeah, baby!)

Equally important to know is that today's game can still be beaten, still sports a low percentage, and can even swing to a negative percentage (in the players' favor) if you use the right strategy, which you indeed will find in this chapter. You'll also have some traps to avoid, such as continuous shuffling machines that take all the fun out of card counting. And you'll need to do some serious shopping for the best playing conditions you can find. For example, you'll want to find the best payouts for making a blackjack—some casinos today have cut the payoff for a player blackjack from 3 to 2 to a lowly 6 to 5. And you thought only players were greedy?

Before we delve into the secrets of beating this ever-changing game, let's be sure you understand the rules you'll most likely find in casinos today, and confirm the correct player options to exercise. Here's a concise rundown—certainly couldn't hurt to review it, right?

HOW TO PLAY THE GAME

Standard-issue playing cards (with jokers removed) are dealt from a **shoe** (a box containing four or more decks) or by hand (usually one or two decks) to each player and the dealer, each getting two cards. One of the dealer's cards is dealt face up for everyone to see, while the other card is dealt face down. The number cards count as face value, the **picture** cards (kings, queens and jacks) count as 10, and the ace is counted as either 1 or 11, whichever is better to make or approach 21. The four suits have no significance.

The idea is to beat the dealer by either holding a hand that's closer to 21 than the dealer's hand (neither hand can exceed 21), or by holding any hand in which the dealer exceeds 21 by drawing additional cards. The strategy for playing your hand in optimum fashion will be clearly spelled out for you in the following pages.

You may **hit** (ask for an additional card) as many times as you like, until you **stand** (are finished). If you take too many cards and exceed 21, it's an automatic **bust**, and you immediately lose. Toss your cards on the table between the betting area and the dealer to indicate the bust. The dealer will remove your wager. In most casinos today, all the player's cards are dealt face up, so you never need to touch the cards, and shouldn't. In this case, when you bust, the dealer will remove your cards (and your wager) for you.

When all players at the table have acted on their hands, the dealer turns over his **hole** card, the card that was dealt face down, and stands only if the total is 17 or more. He is required to draw cards until the hand totals at least 17 or more. If the dealer busts in the process, all players who did not bust are automatic and immediate winners.

If, however, the dealer does not bust and has a hand that totals between 17 and 21—which it must, because the dealer draws to make at least 17, and more than 21 is a bust—the hand is compared to yours to see which is closer to 21. Whichever is closer wins. If both you and the dealer have the same total, it's called a **push** (a tie) and there's no decision on the bet. In that case, you are free to remove your wager, increase it, or decrease it. Only after a push or after a win can you again touch the chips in your betting area. Never touch your bet after a game has begun and before the hand is settled. Casino personnel are very suspicious.

Read this brief section again carefully until you fully understand it. It's the essence of the game! If you're wondering on what hand totals to draw cards, or at what point to stop drawing, don't worry about it now. We'll cover that later for all possible hand combinations.

All bets that win are paid at even money. If you bet $5, you win $5, and so on. However, if your first two cards are a 10-value card and an ace, it's called a **blackjack** (wins outright) and is paid at 3 to 2. If you bet $10, you'll receive $15 in winnings! The 10-value card does not need to be a picture card: A 10 or any other suit is worth just as much as a jack, queen, or king. *Any* 10-value card and an ace make a blackjack.

Note that in recent years, many casinos have begun paying only 6 to 5 on blackjacks, meaning a $10 bet returns only $12, as opposed to $15 when the table pays 3 to 2. Obviously, you would rather play in casinos offering the 3 to 2 bonus on blackjacks!

If the dealer receives a blackjack on the first two cards, you lose at **even money** (only the amount of your wager) unless you also have a blackjack, in which case it's a push.

The only other exception to the even-money wagers is called **insurance**. Here's how it works: If the dealer's upcard is an ace, the dealer will ask all the players if they wish to take insurance. To do that, you bet an additional amount up to one-half of your original wager, betting that the dealer does in fact have a 10-value card underneath, in which case your side-bet wins at 2 to 1 odds. The bottom line on insurance is don't do it! It's a silly bet that only increases the house percentage.

HIT OR STAND MOTIONS

To recap, the most important option you have is to either hit or stand. Your way of indicating to the dealer that you wish to hit or stand depends on whether the cards are dealt face up or face down. Although virtually all casinos today deal the player's cards face up, a few casinos still deal the player's first two cards face down, as was common many years ago, so I'll cover both scenarios.

At tables where the cards are dealt face up, you should never touch the cards. To signal a hit, you can make either of two motions. I prefer to point at the cards, actually touching the table with my finger about two to three inches from the cards. This way, there's no question that I want another card. Unfortunately, some casinos frown on this action for whatever illogical reason. The other motion is to simply bring your hand toward you in a scooping motion. Just be sure you do this over the table so that the "eye in the sky" can see it to record. (The casino's video cameras are there to protect both the casino and the player. Don't be intimidated by them.)

If you don't want another card, I recommend that you simply put out your hand toward the dealer, as if to indicate "stop." The casino recommends a horizontal motion as if you're wiping a piece of glass above the table. However, it's been my experience that the latter motion can easily be confused with the opposite signal, especially if a player is particularly sloppy with the motions. Try it my way.

At tables where the cards are dealt face down, you obviously must pick up the cards to read your hand. If you do not want another card, simply place both cards face down on the table and slightly under your bet. In most casinos, it's all right to simply place the cards within close proximity of your wager. If you want a hit, keep the cards in your hand until it's your turn to play. Then, lightly scrape the card edges on the table, toward you.

Incidentally, it makes no difference whether the cards are dealt face down or face up in blackjack. This isn't poker! But it does make a significant difference if you're counting cards, which we'll discuss later.

SPLITTING

Another important option for you is to **split** identical cards in your original hand, such as a pair of 8s. When this option is available, you do not just automatically do it! The decision to split or not to split your pair depends on whether or not it will be an advantage to you. When we get to the basic strategy section later on, I'll detail each possible pair combination in comparison to the dealer's upcard, and tell you the optimum decision you should make.

For now, let's prematurely make two important rules abundantly clear. Even if you're an inexperienced player, you can probably understand the solid reasoning behind these rules.

1. **Never ever split 10-value cards such as two face cards, and never split 5's and 4's.**
    Splitting 10-value cards is my favorite example of greed. You're throwing away an excellent hand! Players who split a 20 should have their heads examined.
2. **Always split aces and 8's**

When you wish to split your cards at a face-down table, simply position your cards face up and behind your bet (to the dealer's side). Then make another wager of the same size and place it directly beside (not on top of) your original bet. At a face-up table, you only need to make a new bet inside the betting circle to indicate the split, since your cards are already in position.

Tell the dealer you wish to split the pair, and you will be given two more cards, one to each card you split, creating two new hands that are working for you. If you receive another identical card, some casinos allow you to split again, and you'll have three hands in play. However, most casinos today do not allow the re-splitting of aces. To make matters worse, the hands stand after the dealer has given one card to each of the split aces. The casino will not afford you the option of hitting. Regardless, splitting aces is a strong player advantage. Always do it.

DOUBLE DOWN

Here's an option that figures significantly in your ability to adjust the percentages. You may **double down** on your first two cards—that is, you can make an additional bet up to the amount of your original wager and receive only one card (one hit) from the dealer.

Obviously, the time to double down is when you have a hand total of 10 or 11 and the dealer's upcard is 6 or less. That's the ideal situation. Another 10-value card will give you a 20 or 21. Even a 7, 8, or 9 will give you a pat hand (17 or better). That's the reason I told you earlier never to split 5s. The two 5-value cards give you a hand total of 10, and that's usually a good time to double down. I'll give you the complete basic strategy for doubling down, and all the other player options later on. You'll know exactly when to do it and when not to.

As I've mentioned before, the casino industry has been negligent in its efforts to standardize game rules. Perhaps it's an element of competition that shouldn't be standardized. Just remember that the rules do vary, and doubling down is a good example. Some casinos limit doubling down to only 10 or 11. Still other casinos will allow doubling down on any two cards, and that's a big advantage to the player, as you'll learn later. Unfortunately, most casinos not only have different rules, they change their rules about as often as your gas bill goes up. The best policy is to simply ask before you play.

SURRENDER

This is an option that few players understand or readily use, probably because many casinos no longer offer it. If you are fortunate to play in a casino where **surrender** is available, this is what it means to you: If you don't like your first two cards (and that happens a lot) you can surrender the hand and lose only one-half of your bet. To surrender, simply state "surrender" to the dealer and throw in your cards. The dealer will remove half of your bet and you're out of the woods. It's that simple.

There was a time when I refused to play blackjack in any casino without surrender rules. Who wants to hit a 15 or 16 against the dealer's 10? Years ago, a player could surrender before the peek: It was called "early surrender" and casinos promoted it to attract players. The rule was rather rudely downgraded in later years to "late surrender," where a player could only surrender after the peek. Suffice it to say that casinos today are getting all the players they need without it.

A SOFT HAND

Any hand that includes an ace has two values—a **soft** value and a **hard** value. If your hand is an A-6, the soft value is 17 (counting the ace as 11), and the hard value is 7 (counting the ace as 1).

A soft 19 or 20 is good enough and you should stand. But there's a decision to make whether or not to hit a soft 17 or 18, although it doesn't come up that often. It's important to remember that a soft hand, such as a soft 17, will not bust. A 10-value card will simply make the soft 17 hard. Depending on the dealer's upcard, you actually may want to double down on a soft 17 if the casino allows you to do it. I'll give you the basic strategy for soft hands in the following pages.

Earlier in this chapter, I told you that the dealer is required to draw to 16 and stand on 17. That's the basic rule on the Strip in Las Vegas and in most other major casinos across the country. However, many casinos in Northern Nevada and downtown Las Vegas, and some Indian casinos, require the dealer to hit a soft 17. It's a nasty ploy, and definitely a disadvantage to the player.

Look on the table layout before you play. It should clearly state, "The dealer must draw to 16 and stand on all 17's." Much better!

BASIC STRATEGY

Before we look at the charts, let's apply some good old-fashioned horse sense and see if we can understand the reasoning behind the strategies. You'll be able to remember these strategies more easily if you understand why they work!

First, let's identify the potential bust hands as **stiffs**—and that's a great term for them. When the dealer gives you a hard, unpaired 12, 13, 14, 15, or 16, you got stiffed! If your hand is 15 or 16 (other than 8-8), you've got one of the two worst hands possible; and it's especially tough if the dealer's upcard is a 7 or higher. Don't screw it up any more than it already is by not hitting it, or by not surrendering it if you can.

If your cards total 17, 18, 19, or 20, it's a **pat** hand. It's decent. Although 17 and 18 may be good enough to stand on, they certainly won't get all the marbles all the time. Blackjacks, 20, and 19 are the real goodies you're looking for.

Judging by what we now understand to be the object of the game, and the basic game rules themselves, it would appear that the biggest casino advantage is the fact that the player has to draw before the dealer does. That simple fact accounts for a hefty 7 percent advantage to the house. Sensing that problem, many inexperienced players elect to never hit a stiff for fear of busting. That dumb little ploy is worth about 3 percent to the house. We can decrease the house's 7 percent advantage other ways, but not that way!

To make matters worse, some casinos that offer a single-deck or double-deck game are now paying only 6 to 5 for a blackjack. Most casinos dealing six or eight decks have retained the 3 to 2 payoff. If you don't get 3 to 2 for a blackjack, don't play! The 3 to 2 payoff reduces the house advantage from 7 percent to a little under 5 percent. Perfectly executed player options based on basic strategy (including hitting, standing, doubling, and splitting for both hard and soft hands) will lower the house percentage to about 1/2 percent, though this number cannot be determined precisely because of variations in rules.

Now, see if you can identify the good cards and the bad cards for the player. It's important. Think about it. It seems obvious that all 10-value cards are good because they help give you 20s, and pair up nicely with an ace for a blackjack. Sure, 10-value cards are good, but what about 2s, 3s, 4s, 5s, and 6s? They help to promote those lousy stiffs, right? And more important, they can improve a dealer's stiff hand. Therefore, 2s, 3s, 4s, 5s, and 6s are indeed bad cards.

Although we're getting a little ahead of ourselves, the object of card counting is to determine how many 10-value cards and how many small cards are left in the deck, based on how many you've seen played. When the ratio of 10-value cards to small cards is high, you have an advantage. If there are too many small cards left in the deck, the casino has a distinct advantage.

The strategies that follow are very powerful, but understand that no strategy will help you win if you don't help yourself. Knowledge is power. But poor play on your part—reckless, senseless betting—can destroy that power in no time. Do yourself a favor: Read *What Casinos Don't Want You To Know*, a perfect complement to this book. The chapters on money management and common-sense betting will add a new and vital dimension to your game. Still, the most powerful strategies in the world are useless to you if you aren't disciplined.

> Discipline is the most powerful strategy of all!

PLAYING STRATEGIES
HIT-OR-STAND STRATEGY FOR STIFFS

PLAYER'S HARD HAND	DEALER'S UP-CARD									
	2	3	4	5	6	7	8	9	10	A
16										
15										
14		STAND						HIT		
13										
12	HIT									

ALWAYS STAND ON 17 OR BETTER

Our strategy for hitting or standing with stiffs is really quite simple:

1. **Always hit a stiff when the dealer has a 7 or higher.**
   Remember it as 7-UP and you'll never forget it.
2. **Always stand on a stiff when the dealer has 6 or less showing, except when you have 12.**
   The dealer does not have a pat hand (with the exception of A-6), so there is a good possibility the dealer will bust.
3. **Always stand on 17 or better.**
   Never, even in your wildest dreams, hit 17! Dealers must alert pit bosses in many casinos when a player hits 17 or better. See if you can guess why.
4. **Always draw a card on 11 or less.**
   You might actually double down or split depending on the card values, but at the very least, you'll always hit it.

Incidentally, the hit-and-stand rules apply not only to your original hand but to your hand at any time. For example, if your original hand is 10-4 against the dealer's 10, you hit it. You receive a 2. Now you have 16. According to the chart, you must continue hitting until you have 17 or better. Sure, the odds are against you, but you had a losing hand in the first place. Over the long term, you'll reduce the casino's initial advantage that we talked about by about 2.5 percent with correct hitting and standing strategy.

Reducing the percentages against you is the name of the game!

HARD DOUBLE-DOWN STRATEGY

PLAYER'S HARD HAND	DEALER'S UP-CARD									
	2	3	4	5	6	7	8	9	10	A
11		D O U B L E								
10		D O W N								
9									H I T	

1. **Always double down on 11, regardless of the dealer's upcard.**

2. **Double down on 10 only when the dealer's upcard is 9 or lower.**

   If the dealer's upcard is a 10 or an ace, it's obviously too risky.

3. **Double down on 9 only when the dealer's upcard is 3, 4, 5, or 6.**

   However, this is a moot point in many casinos where doubling is limited to 10 or 11. Doubling after you have split is equally restricted in many casinos. Ask before you play to be sure you understand the rules in a particular casino. Always seek out the best playing conditions.

Proper strategy for hard double downs (and for soft doubling, which we'll cover later) further reduces the casino percentage by about 1.5 percent. We're getting there!

SPLITTING STRATEGY

PLAYER'S HAND	DEALER'S UP-CARD									
	2	3	4	5	6	7	8	9	10	A
A-A				S P L I T						
10-10				S T A N D						
9-9										
8-8			S P L I T							
7-7										
6-6										
5-5			D O U B L E							
4-4								H I T		
3-3	H I T		S P L I T							
2-2										

1. **Always split aces and 8's. Never split 10's, 5's or 4's.**
   Treat 5-5 as 10 and follow our double-down rule—double if the dealer shows 9 or less; otherwise, just hit.
2. **Split 9's when the dealer has 9 or less.**
3. **Split 7's when the dealer has 7 or less.**
4. **Split 6's when the dealer has 6 or less.**
   Remember that the dealer's upcard is always the same or less than the card you're splitting with 9's, 7's, and 6's.
5. **Only split 3's and 2's when the dealer's upcard is 4, 5, 6, or 7.**
   Otherwise, just hit.

SOFT-HAND STRATEGY

PLAYER'S SOFT HAND	DEALER'S UP-CARD									
	2	3	4	5	6	7	8	9	10	A
A-9 (20)										
A-8 (19)				S T A N D						
A-7 (18)										
A-6 (17)										
A-5 (16)										
A-4 (15)	H I T		D O U B L E						H I T	
A-3 (14)										
A-2 (13)										

1. **Always stand on a soft 19 and 20.**
   They represent good hands, regardless of the dealer's upcard.

2. **Always double down on a soft 13 through 18 when the dealer has 4, 5, or 6 showing.**
   Of course, you can only double down on a soft 13 if the rules allow it. Otherwise, hit 13 through 17.

3. **Always double down on a soft 18 when the dealer is showing 4, 5, or 6; and hit when the dealer is showing 9, 10, or ace.**
   A soft 18 is the most difficult to remember because there are three options. When the dealer has a 9 or higher upcard, he may have a better hand, so it does pay to try to improve your soft 18. Remember, you can't bust any soft hand with a single hit. However, if you end up with a poor draw such as a 5, you must hit it again (hard 13) and take your chances.

SURRENDER STRATEGY

The rules for surrender are so simple that we don't need a graphic chart to show you.

PLAYER'S HAND	DEALER'S UPCARD
15-16 (hard)	7-8-9-10-A

Surrender a 15 or 16 stiff (except 8-8) when the dealer has a 7 or higher upcard, if you're playing in a casino where it is allowed. Surrender is worth nearly one percent to you, so look for it—but don't expect to find it in one-casino markets. This rule is generally offered as a casino marketing tool in competitive venues, assuming there are empty tables to fill. Don't hesitate to lose half of your bet with a bad hand. Sure beats losing it all!

BASIC STRATEGY CARDS: A SMART WAY TO PLAY

It's not as tough to apply basic strategy today as it was years ago. Today we have strategy cards for all the casino games, and they have been approved by nearly all casinos for players to use at the tables. A blackjack basic strategy card shows every dealer upcard and player hand combination. The card tells you what to do. There is no guesswork.

A strategy card for blackjack offers a great benefit to players in the sense that only one strategy card is needed for all the game variants, including the number of decks in play, from one deck to eight decks. Other cards on the market designated for a certain game variation may only serve to confuse most players, wondering if they've chosen the right card. With the Gollehon strategy card for blackjack, you always know you've got the right card!

It's best to memorize the right moves, but let's be realistic. Some players are only occasional players. They can't be expected to remember all the player options and perform flawlessly during those twice-a-year trips to Vegas. For such players, strategy cards are a godsend, but I'm sure you're wondering why casinos allow their use. Simple. The cards speed up the games. There's no pondering, no hair twirling, no looking up to the heavens for help—it's all right there in front of you. There's absolutely no reason to slow down the game. Yes, casinos love these cards. The more hands played, the more the casino makes. It's that simple.

I hope you didn't think that all you had to do was get your hands on a good basic strategy card and you could tell your boss what he could do with your crummy job. Not quite. As good as these cards are, they are not going to wipe out all the casinos. With the way the game is being played today in most venues, correct basic strategy will reduce the house percentage to a little less than one-half percent, a nearly even game.

BEYOND THE BASICS

Blackjack is a game of patience. The key is waiting for the right opportunities—and that's why you need to be patient before you even sit down. Don't rush to play! The top players I know watch a table, maybe several tables, for as long as it takes before they decide to play. The term they like to use for this maneuver is called *drifting*, meaning that they're getting a drift for the tables.

Now let's talk about you for a moment. When you've finally found a spot, do you feel relieved, happy to get off your feet and settled in? Most players do. But that doesn't work either. Top players never think in terms of settling in. They're never settled, not by any stretch. It's an interesting dichotomy of discipline: Pro players have the patience to seek out what appears to be a "receptive" table, but they have no patience at all if they are rudely welcomed. They sit on the edge of their chairs fully prepared to escape quickly if the table turns into an ambush.

When I used to give talks on casino games, blackjack was always the game that drew the greater audiences. I started each discussion by asking a question about table conditions. I would identify a condition that is increasingly becoming the standard fare, no matter the casino, no matter the venue—full tables, even on weekdays. The question would usually stump the audience. Here's what I asked: "Let's say the casino is crowded. You want to play but all the tables are full. You've spotted a guy ready to leave a table because he just lost all of his money. But why would you want to take his place?"

The top players I know take the same stance about playing conditions as I do. For example, if a dealer is particularly strong, making pat hands out of stiffs and basically cleaning out the players, I see it as a trend, not an anomaly. Regardless of the game, seasoned players believe that trends are strangely stubborn and tend not to change in some remarkably quick fashion. Smart players go with the trends. Smart players would never sit themselves down at such a dangerous table. Sure, there could be a sudden change in fortune, but what do you think is more likely to happen? If you don't investigate before you play, you won't even know if there is a trend to monitor.

The first thing to do when you decide to play blackjack is *not* to play for a while—not until you've found a spot that seems safe. And if the casino is so busy that you can't really do any serious shopping for table conditions, you're in the wrong casino! Or you've picked a time to play when it's too busy. Are you just going to wait it out, grab the first open chair and play? I hope not. I would like to think that this discussion has tempered your anxiety to play, which is another advantage of table shopping. No one should play when they're in an anxious state, under the gun, and feeling pressure. Learn how to enjoy the time before you play. It should be a time of anticipation, not anxiety. Use it wisely.

Most players think that the essence of the game is to either get to 21 or get closer to 21 than the dealer—but that's not exactly true. In fact, it's a common misread right out of the starting gate. Far too many players simply misunderstand the workings of the game.

> The real essence of blackjack is simply to beat the dealer!

Even if you win by doubling down on a soft 17 and end up making a mess of it, who cares? A win is a win! Do you think that someone takes points away from you because you won with a weak hand? Or gives you points because you boldly smacked a 16, even though you ended up doing a belly flop? Hey, this isn't Olympic diving. There's no scoring to worry about. The idea is to win, regardless of how you get there.

Forget about drawing to 21 or always making a pat hand. And take that fear of busting out of your head too. Players who live by this misconception tend to make two critical mistakes: First, some players tend to draw excessively to get that "closest to 21" hand. Even though they may know basic strategy, they chuck the charts and make up their own rules. Second, some players take the opposite approach—not drawing when they should draw—relying too heavily on the dealer's likelihood of busting.

The key to at least having a chance at this game is to follow basic strategy *to the letter*. Never amend the strategy rules to suit your own misguided understanding of how the game is played. Basic strategy needs no special tweaking on your part; it has been proven to be the best approach to beating this game. The mathematical wizards who conquered this game in the

1960s—yes, that long ago—devised basic strategy with what is now time-tested accuracy. It's a testament to the work of these great pioneers of blackjack. You wouldn't dare mess with their work, would you?

If you previously had a little misunderstanding, you've got it straight now, right? Good! Then let's get on to the other aspect of beating blackjack—card counting. And for that, we again credit those elite mathematicians of yesteryear. Boy, talk about getting it right the first time—they were right on the money to help you and generations of players win money.

Here's an absolute given: You must count the cards if you want to have a chance to beat the game over the long term. And here's the good news: The card counting strategy you use does not necessarily need to be complicated. There are easy ones. In fact, the strategy I'm about to give you is clearly the easiest and most effective. That's right—I'm going to give you your cake and you can eat it, too! Card counting is the hallmark of any blackjack strategy.

Card counting is one of the few strategies that casinos actually fear. Knowing that played cards affect the distribution of future cards is the essence of card counting. If there were strategy cards for counting cards, the casinos wouldn't allow them. No chance, so don't bother looking for any. Why won't the casinos allow card-counting strategy cards? You can answer that one yourself: A good card counter practicing basic strategy can take that minuscule percentage away from the casinos— steal it right from under their noses and then turn it against them.

If you're going to do some fancy counting, you're going to have to do it in your head. But don't let the idea of having to do all this counting stuff in your head scare you away. New strategies have been created, refined from older methods that were too complicated anyhow, that are far easier to learn.

THE IMPERIAL II COUNT STRATEGY

One of the neatest card counting strategies is what I call the Imperial II Count. It's a modernization of one of my earliest strategies that was based on an overview of played cards. It seems almost too simple to work, but it does. First, let me give you the basics behind the Imperial II Count so that you can understand the underlying principles. You'll be able to play it more efficiently if you understand how and why it works.

Most all casino blackjack tables today are played full or nearly so. Years ago, you could always find an open table and play the dealer heads up, one on one. And many of the older strategies, such as my original Imperial Count, were designed for just that situation. But it's become increasingly difficult to have a one-on-one confrontation with a dealer today. Why? Well, we can look to the airlines for the answer. How many planes fly full today? The answer is: All of them.

Casinos have decided to run their games with the same economics in mind. There are few, if any, open tables because open tables are not making money. On weekends, it's even tough to find open seats! Casinos have wised up and, like the airlines, now force their customers to play musical chairs. It seems as if every time you look for a seat, there are three available and four players who want them. So, for a card counting strategy to be useful today, it must work at a full table of seven players—a perfect number for the Imperial II Count.

Another sign of the times is multiple-deck shoes. Outside of Nevada, your chances of finding a single-deck or two-deck game are slim and none—and slim just left town. There's no question about it, a good strategy today must be designed for multiple decks, particularly an eight-deck shoe. Eight decks is a perfect number for the Imperial II Count. Virtually all multiple-deck games today are dealt with the cards face up, which is an important consideration for card counting. How can you count them if you can't see them?

Full tables, multiple decks, cards face up. So far, so good!

Knowing that the small cards—2, 3, 4, 5, and 6—are bad cards for players, keeping a count of these cards (and only these cards) is the centerpiece of the Imperial II Count. The 10-value cards and the ace are the good cards for players, but we don't have to keep track of them because the Imperial II Count is a balanced count (five small-card values vs. five good-card values—A-K-Q-J-10). Keeping track of both good and bad cards would be redundant.

The more small cards that are removed from the shoe the better. Ideally, the small cards should leave the shoe at a higher than normal exit rate, and that's what the Imperial II Count does: It measures the rate at which the small cards are played.

To make the Imperial II Count work best for you, always position yourself at **third base**, the seat at the far left of the table, so that you can see as many played cards as possible before you act on your hand. If there are seven players at the table, you will see an average of 21 cards per deal—including yours, all hits, and the dealer's upcard. Based on the ratio of small cards to all other cards, eight of these cards should be small ones. Simply count these small cards as you see them. If you count ten of them after the first deal, there's a slight player advantage. If you count six, there's a slight additional edge for the casino.

There's one obvious glitch in this strategy that needs to be accounted for. The counting procedure I just outlined—looking for eight small cards out of a 21-card average—is based on the dealer's upcard being 7 or higher. If the dealer's upcard is one of the small cards you're tracking—2, 3, 4, 5, or 6—then you must adjust your card average downward, accounting for fewer player hits, with the net result that you will only be looking for seven small cards. (Remember to count the dealer's small card, too, so you'll only be looking for six small cards among the players at a full table.)

If the table only has six players, you need to make another adjustment. With a dealer upcard of 7 or higher, look for seven small cards. If the dealer's upcard is one of the small cards you're tracking, look for five more small cards. If the table has fewer than six players, avoid it. If the table where you're playing has six players and loses a player, move to another table with more players. Remember, you want as many players as possible in order to see as many cards as possible.

IMPERIAL II COUNT STRATEGY

DEALER'S UPCARD: 7 THRU ACE		DEALER'S UPCARD: 2 THRU 6	
# OF PLAYERS	SMALL CARDS	# OF PLAYERS	SMALL CARDS
7	8	7	7
6	7	6	6

If you're interested in the exact mathematics of how we arrived at these numbers, here's some technical information for you. Otherwise, just take my word for it and skip this paragraph. The value of 21 cards per deal to seven hands is based on an average of 2.857 cards per hand when the dealer's upcard is 7 or higher, and 2.280 cards per hand when the dealer's upcard is 2 through 6. The values are based on actual casino studies. Computer models, based on perfect basic strategy and the widely used new standard for game rules, show these values to be somewhat higher. The deviations are most likely due to player-option errors resulting in lower hit frequencies. The numbers listed for "small cards" are simply the product of .3846 (small-card expectancy) and the cards-per-hand averages plus 1 (the dealer's upcard), times the number of players. The effects of rounded values should be negligible in the short term.

KEEPING THE COUNT

Perhaps the neatest feature of the Imperial II Count is the way you actually keep a record of the rate of small cards appearing. I recommend using a chip as your means of recording the results. Choose a part of the chip's artwork to act as an hour hand, as if the chip is a clock face. Point the hand at 12 o'clock (straight up) to indicate a neutral count. As your count moves up in a favorable direction, simply turn the chip so that the hand is pointing to the right, perhaps at one o'clock. If the count is heading in a unfavorable direction, move the hand to the left.

The incremental turn of the chip is something you'll have to tweak for yourself, but it has to be relative to the degree with which you are seeing the small cards removed from the deck. Most of the time, you'll count the normal number of small cards for a particular deal, so you would not turn your chip. I only turn the chip a full hour's worth, for example, when I see a deal with a significant fluctuation from the norm of, say, three or four cards. I've played this new version of the Imperial Count for about two years, and I've never been in a position where the hand was pointing past five o'clock. Since the right half of the chip is positive and the left half is negative, so to speak, you should not move the hand beyond six o'clock.

USING YOUR NEW SKILLS

Just keeping the count is one thing. Using it is another. So how do you use it? It's easy: Simply use your count to adjust the size of your wagers. Make larger wagers when the count is player-favorable. Make smaller wagers when the count is running against you. I don't like making hard-and-fast rules, but the following chart should help you in structuring your wagers. Use it only as a guide.

BET AMOUNTS

NON-FAVORABLE			FAVORABLE		
COUNT	HAND	BET	COUNT	HAND	BET
0	NOON	TM	3	1 PM	2X
3	11 AM	TM	6	2 PM	3X
6	10 AM	EXIT	9	3 PM	5X

TM stands for Table Minimum.
Hand refers to the hour locations on a clock face.

The wager amounts in the chart are to show a bet spread relationship only, and are not suggestive of specific dollar amounts. Wagers should never exceed the table minimum if values are not well within the right side of the clock. Change tables when the values have stagnated on the left side of the clock.

If you're relatively new to this game, you might have already realized the second advantage of card counting. That's right, there are two. You now know that card counting helps you by telling you when to bet more, when to bet less, and when not to bet at all. But did you know that it also helps you by telling you when to alter basic strategy? It's such an obvious feature that we really don't need a chart to explain it.

For example, if you are dealt a 10-6—a likely bust hand—and the dealer is showing 9, basic strategy says you should hit that stiff. Ideally, you would like to know that there is an excess of small-value cards remaining to be played. But what if your count indicates that there is actually a deficiency of small cards remaining? A deficiency of small cards most likely means an excess of 10-value cards. In that case, you certainly don't want a 10-value card, so you alter basic strategy and stand instead of hit.

Good card counters who are playing in ideal conditions can detect those times when the edge has moved across the table.

And for that fleeting moment, they've done something that other players at other games can't do—predict opportunity.

When I talked about sizing up blackjack tables at the top of this chapter, I didn't mention the number of decks being played because you weren't ready for it then, but you are now. Look for the fewest decks being played. Eight decks are the worst, six decks are a little better, one-deck and two-deck games are the best. (Single-deck and double-deck games are where you'll most likely find the short payoff for a blackjack. Remember that if you can't get a 3 to 2 payoff for a blackjack, don't play.)

Most players think that the introduction of multiple-deck shoes to the blackjack scene was merely to cut down on the number of shuffles, thus giving the casinos more decisions per hour, which is what they want. I'm sure that was a factor, but it wasn't the overriding reason for this major change to the game. Multiple decks of cards tend to smooth out fluctuations. In other words, more decks produce a more random distribution of cards. There is less likelihood that small cards, for example, will clump together within the shoe. Now you've got it: The changeover to multiple decks was just another strike against card counting, and a very effective one indeed. In fact, the use of multiple decks takes away some of the advantages of both basic strategy and card counting. A six-deck or eight-deck shoe can easily cost players half of a percent.

If you saw four aces removed from a one-deck game during the early deals, you can bet your bottom dollar that you won't see any more for the remainder of the deck. But if you saw four aces removed from an eight-deck shoe, the absence of those four aces, although significant, is far less significant.

The effects of early anomalies in an eight-deck shoe are clearly not as dramatic as the effects on a single or double deck. It's all based on what mathematicians call *dilution*. That is, the more cards to select from, the less likely certain cards will pair up. It explains the unusual drop in frequency of blackjacks, for example. Expect more from a single deck; expect less proportionally from an eight-deck shoe. Clearly, a multiple-deck game presents problems with or without continuous shufflers.

Yet another contributor to this strange phenomenon is called *entropy*, a mathematical term that explains the tendency of objects to move away from their original order. You can understand it best by visualizing a jar half full of jellybeans with all the red ones on the bottom and the black ones on top. The more you shake the jar, the more dispersed the beans become. You would never be able to reverse this disorder by further shaking. You wouldn't expect them to ever reassemble with the reds on the bottom and the black ones on top. But if we used only a few beans instead of half the jar, we would have a chance (although we might not have the time) to restore the original order.

And so it goes with the shoe games in casinos throughout the world. Today, casino bosses want to see lots and lots of cards on the blackjack tables moving further and further away from order through shuffle after shuffle. That's right: The cards are continually moving toward chaos—chaos for the card counter.

LOOKING AT THE BRIGHT SIDE

Sure, being a card counter is not what it used to be, but that doesn't mean it isn't worth doing. Let me tell you how I play blackjack, what I look for, and what I settle for. First and foremost, I can't play against a continuous shuffler. I want to count cards; in fact, I enjoy it. But a continuous shuffler makes the effort a waste of time. Incidentally, don't think that all shuffling machines are continuous. Many casinos use machines that shuffle a number of decks separate from the decks in play. That's different, and that's okay.

Knowing that it's nearly impossible for me to find a single-deck game with a full payoff for a blackjack—given the casino markets I'm close to—I give up the half percent for multiple decks instead of giving up nearly three times that figure for the short 6 to 5 blackjack payoff at a hand-held game (one or two decks). I need full double-down privileges, and I need a reasonable cut-card penetration. If more than one-and-one-half decks are cut out of an eight-deck shoe, I'll pass. Some casinos cut more than two full decks! To a card counter, taking such a high percentage of cards out of play is a slap in the face.

There is a bright side to the issue of card dispersion that we just talked about. As it relates to casino games, the *permeation* of cards is the term more popularly used, and it's not just at blackjack, but other card games as well—baccarat and even Texas hold'em, for example.

Is there a flip side to the "disorder" theory of mixing? Is there an inherent flaw in the shuffling of cards by hand? A poker player would ask if there's a predictable element to the selection of community cards, for example. If two aces are tossed into the pile together, might they stay together for the next deal?

As a side note to this discussion, without an interest in card-distribution anomalies, the seemingly never-ending list of casino-imposed drawbacks can take a player out of the game. In fact, today I play mostly Texas hold'em and craps when I feel the anticipation, relegating blackjack to the back burner. But a recent study of deck-construction components has perked my interest, and I include this material here in the hope that it will perk yours, too. Now, let's get back to the question at hand.

The question really is this: Exactly how thorough is a good shuffling?

This novel question should not be taken lightly. Card values are clumped before the seal is broken on a new deck. The cards run in numerical order; the face cards, for example, are grouped together. When multiple decks are used, the dealers scoop up the cards in such a way that the face cards of one deck actually clump with another. Test the theory yourself. Stack a deck with all four cards of any same value placed anywhere in the deck. Shuffle the heck out of them and see how they were dispersed. You might be very surprised.

In fact, experts who study the randomness of selection in casino games (the keno hopper and roulette wheel bias are the most mentioned examples) believe that a perfectly random shuffle is all but impossible. (The jury's still out on continuous shuffling machines.) This is why I said earlier that I no longer mind going up against multiple decks at the blackjack tables as much as I mind many of the other casino countermeasures.

I've fought tougher battles in the casino trenches—and I'm still fighting!

3 ATTACKING THE CASINO AT CRAPS

The dice tables in the casino are where you'll often find unfettered excitement. You can hear the cheers from the far reaches of the largest casino floors. Some seasoned players probably would say that you don't hear it often enough, and I would probably concur. Craps is known for its streakiness, if there is such a word. Streaks of hot and cold test the mettle of the toughest players trying to outguess the dice. But when those infamous hot streaks do happen, the casino bosses tend to get a little worried. Really! Depending on who's at the table—high rollers or low rollers—a hot run of winning numbers could cost the casino hundreds of thousands of dollars, maybe even millions.

Some players win a few hundred thousand, others win a few hundred. It's like a dice dealer told me years ago: "Players don't react quickly enough and they don't bet enough during a hot streak." It's absolutely true. But I have yet to find anyone who can accurately point out when a table is about to get hot.

The excitement of craps—*noisy* excitement—means players are winning. It beckons more players as well as potential players who just watch because they're afraid to jump in. Let's hope this chapter will clear the air about this game's unfortunate stigma. I hear it all the time: "Craps is complicated." And when I hear it, I know that I'm listening to someone who doesn't play. Why? Because craps isn't the least bit complicated—it's almost as easy as playing slots. Really!

You don't need to know the odds on your winning bets, though most players want to know them to make sure the dealers are paying them correctly. And you don't even need to know most of the bets, because most craps bets are not the smart bets to make anyhow. There are only three bets to make, and two of them are virtually identical—they're just made at different times, that's all—so, we're talking two bets. Does that sound complicated?

Let's learn the game, uncover some secrets, and make some serious money!

HOW TO PLAY THE GAME

First let's consider the dice. There are two dice in play, with each cube having six sides, 1 through 6. That means that numbers from 2 through 12 can be made when two dice are rolled. Let's make an important distinction right now: The odds of rolling these 11 numbers vary. The odds of rolling a 4, for example, are much higher (harder) than rolling a 7. There are only three ways you can roll a 4 (2-2, 1-3, and 3-1); there are six ways you can roll a 7 (2-5, 5-2, 1-6, 6-1, 3-4, and 4-3).

THE PASS-LINE BET

Let's list the numbers somewhat out of order so that you can best see what the numbers mean for the most common dice wager, the **pass-line** bet. Here are the numbers in groups for you to remember. Always think of the numbers exactly as I've separated them.

2-3-12	7-11	4-10	5-9	6-8
Craps (Loser)	Natural (Winner)	Point numbers (Must be repeated to win)		

NOTE: Remember the point numbers in pairs as I've listed them. You'll find out why later in this chapter.

1. **Each of the numbers 2, 3, and 12 is called a "craps."**
   Any craps is a loser on the first roll, which is called the **come-out roll**, for all bets on the pass line.
2. **Each of the numbers 7 and 11 is called a "natural."**
   A natural is a winner on the come-out roll.
3. **The remaining numbers—4, 5, 6, 8, 9, and 10—are called "point" numbers.**
   When one of these numbers is rolled on the come-out roll, that same number must be rolled again before a 7 is rolled in order to win the pass-line bet.
4. **A new come-out roll always follows a pass-line decision, win or lose.**
   If a 7 rolls on the come-out roll, the pass line wins. If a 3 rolls on the come-out roll, the pass line loses. If a 6 rolls on the come-out roll, there is no win-or-lose decision at that moment. The shooter rolls again, and then again, however many times are necessary for either the 6 to repeat (in which case the pass line wins), or for the 7 to roll (in which case the pass line loses). All other numbers are of no significance to the pass-line bet while the shooter is trying to repeat a point number, which is called **rolling for the point**. Now you can see why the 7 sometimes wins and sometimes loses!
5. **If the 7 is thrown on the come-out roll, it wins.**
6. **If the 7 is made while the shooter is rolling for the point, it loses.**
   When 7 is made while the shooter is rolling for the point, it's called a **seven-out**. The dice then pass to the next player, moving in a clockwise direction, and it becomes that player's turn to shoot, starting with a new come-out roll.

7. **As long as a shooter does not seven-out, the shooter retains the dice.**

If it's your turn to shoot and you don't want to shoot, that's fine. Simply tell the dealer to "pass the dice," and then it becomes the next player's chance to shoot. When you become more familiar with the game, I'm sure you'll want to shoot. It's fun. All you have to do is toss the dice to the opposite end of the table from where you're standing, and try to bounce both dice off the far wall of the table. It's easier to lightly toss the dice than it is to roll them, especially if you're standing at the far end of a table. No skill is involved, despite the fact that many dice players believe that there are good shooters and not-so-good shooters. It's all a part of the game, just one of so many unique aspects of craps that makes it so exciting.

Now let's pretend to walk up to a table. Look at the illustration of the table layout.

This is a typical Las Vegas layout, although some newer layouts follow the Atlantic City rule of eliminating the "Big 6 and 8" bets on the corners. It's a silly bet that pays 1 to 1 (even money) if a 6 (or 8) is rolled before a 7. The bet should pay 6 to 5. Even a place-bet on 6 or 8 will pay 7 to 6. Players who bet the Big 6 and 8 are showing their inexperience.

Another variation is the field-bet, where some layouts pay double on **both** the 2 and 12. Others pay triple on **either** the 2 or 12, as shown here (triple on 12). Most new casino venues are using the "Las Vegas" layout.

This layout is typical of Northern Nevada casinos. One of the major differences between the two layouts is the location of the "don't pass" and "don't come" sections. The Las Vegas layout has a section reserved for "don't come." Northern Nevada combines the two bets in one section. The other major difference is the odds expression for "prop bets" in the center of the layout. Notice that the Nevada layout defines the odds payout on a hard 8, for example, as 9 to 1. On the Las Vegas layout, the odds are defined are 10 *for* 1. Both expressions are the same. Odds of 10 for 1 just sound better and may lead unsuspecting players to believe they are getting a better payoff. It's a cheap ploy the casinos should be ashamed of.

Notice that the area marked PASS LINE runs completely around the player sections of the table in order that all players have a spot to make this wager directly in front of them. Also notice that both ends of the table are identical. The right side of the layout is only for players standing at that end of the table. If you're at the left end of the table, you need only concern yourself with that part of the layout.

FOLLOW THE PUCK

When you first walk up to a dice table, how do you know if the shooter is about to make a come-out roll or if the shooter is rolling for the point? The **dealer** at the center of the table controls the movement of the dice with a hooked stick, and will usually alert everyone at the table what's going on. If the shooter is about to make a come-out roll, the dealer will announce that the dice are **coming out**. If the shooter is rolling for the point, the dealer will make that clear also by announcing, "The shooter's point is 8" or by simply saying, "Rolling for 8."

Another way to make this determination is to look at the numbered boxes at the back of the layout and locate the **puck**, a round disk that has a white side and a black side. The white side says ON and the black side says OFF. The puck is about four inches in diameter and looks like a hockey puck, so you'll have no trouble finding it.

Those big boxes at the back of the layout represent the point numbers. At each end of the table, there's a box for the 4, 5, 6, 8, 9, and 10. If the shooter is rolling for the point, the puck will be placed within the box of the point number the shooter is rolling for. When the puck is placed in one of these point boxes, the white side (ON) is up. If the puck is in the box marked SIX, that's the point number the shooter is after.

If the puck has its black side (OFF) showing, it is usually found in an adjacent box marked DON'T COME, which relates to an entirely different bet; however, that's the spot the dealers use to place the puck when the next roll is a come-out roll.

As you might imagine, it's more likely that a shooter will be trying to repeat a point number when you walk up than throwing a string of craps or naturals on a come-out roll. So, the shooter will probably be rolling for the point. But possibly, you timed it perfectly and the shooter is about to make a come-out roll. That's your signal to make a pass-line wager. Incidentally, never make a pass-line bet while the shooter is trying to repeat a point number because then it's a bad bet. I'll tell you why later on.

When the shooter wins, everyone on the pass line wins! Unlike "street" craps, all the players at the dice table are playing against the house, not each other. In gambling jargon, the house is banking the bets.

CRAPS IS A GAME OF ODDS!

The next bet to learn is called an **odds bet**, and is directly associated with the pass-line bet that you now know how to make. But before we can understand the odds bet, we have to learn what odds means, and what the correct odds are at a dice table for all the possible numbers. It's important that you know the odds because it tells you how you will be paid when you win. Knowing the odds is your way of checking the payoff to make sure you were paid correctly.

Probability Chart

NUMBER	WAYS	PROBABILITY	HOW
2	1	35 to 1	1-1
3	2	17 to 1	1-2, 2-1
4	3	11 to 1	2-2, 1-3, 3-1
5	4	8 to 1	1-4, 4-1, 2-3, 3-2
6	5	6.2 to 1	3-3, 2-4, 4-2, 1-5, 5-1
7	6	5 to 1	1-6, 6-1, 2-5, 5-2, 3-4, 4-3
8	5	6.2 to 1	4-4, 2-6, 6-2, 3-5, 5-3
9	4	8 to 1	3-6, 6-3, 4-5, 5-4
10	3	11 to 1	5-5, 4-6, 6-4
11	2	17 to 1	5-6, 6-5
12	1	35 to 1	6-6
	36		

In this Probability Chart, it is readily apparent that there are more ways to roll a 7 than any other number. **Probability** means the same thing as odds. Probability is easy to compute if you have to. We know there are 36 ways to roll the dice, and we know there are six ways to roll a 7. That means there must be 30 ways to *not* roll a 7 (36 minus 6). So our odds of rolling the 7 are 30 to 6. Dividing both numbers by 6 gives us 5 to 1.

The Odds of Rolling a 7

Will Not Happen— **5 to 1** —Will Happen

└─ + ─┘ ── Total Number of Trials = 6

Out of six rolls, one roll should be a 7 and five rolls should be some other number. That's 5 to 1 odds. Notice that I said "should be." The actual results may deviate somewhat over the short term, which is what a smart dice player is looking for— an opportunity when the odds have wavered.

WHO HAS THE ADVANTAGE?

Now that you understand odds at the dice table, let's go back to the pass-line rules and see how you stand. Let's see who has the advantage. We know there are four ways to throw a craps and eight ways to make a 7 or 11. Wait a minute—we have an edge here! You bet we do. The player always has a strong advantage on the come-out roll.

There must be a catch, right? Yes, there is—the point numbers! When the shooter has established a point, the casino gets the edge. But not by much. Again, it's easy to see why. There are six ways to make the 7, but remember that the 7 loses when a shooter is rolling for the point. No point number can be made six ways. Your best chance of rolling a point number before a 7 is if the point is 6 or 8, since both of these numbers can be made five ways.

Never make a pass-line bet after the shooter has established a point number. That's a dumb move! You're giving up the best part of a pass-line wager—the come-out roll—where you have an edge, and you're getting down just at the time when the casino gets the nod. Not too smart!

The next logical question is, "Who has the edge when you take both the come-out roll and rolling for point numbers into account?" Not surprisingly, the casino gets the prize, though it's a cheap one. The casino advantage, overall, is 1.41 percent. This percentage may seem relatively low, but it's actually a significant concern. There are ways to reduce it and you are about to learn how.

Now let me repeat a point I made earlier: Always remember point numbers in pairs! You should now be able to see why we combined the point numbers in our earlier chart—6 and 8, 5 and 9, 4 and 10. They were combined because the ways to make them are the same for both numbers in each pair. Accordingly, when odds are given for any point number, it's always the same for its sister point number in the pair. And that's why it's so important to remember the point numbers in pairs.

THE ODDS BET

Now that we really understand odds, we can learn how to make the important **odds bet**. This wager is made only when the shooter has established a point number. Place your odds bet directly behind the pass-line bet, but not in the pass-line area.

Triple-odds bet placed
outside of the live area.

The casino will allow you to bet an amount that can be more than your pass-line bet. How much more depends on the casino. Some casinos will allow only two-times odds, called **double odds**. Some casinos will let you bet three-times odds, called **triple odds**. The more aggressive casinos may go as high as five-times and even ten-times odds. There are casinos in Las Vegas that often banner their craps odds on their marquee boasting 100-times odds! What's the big deal, you ask?

> The odds bet is a fair bet. The casino doesn't earn a penny on it!

The odds bet is paid at the correct odds of rolling a point number before rolling a 7! Your wager on the pass-line is only paid at even money, regardless of the number. But the odds bet is paid at **true odds**. It is the bet that fortunes are made of!

Here's a chart that gives you the correct odds of repeating point numbers before a 7 rolls. Remember these odds because they tell you how you will be paid if you win.

POINT NUMBER	CORRECT ODDS OF REPEATING BEFORE A 7
6 & 8	6 to 5
5 & 9	3 to 2
4 & 10	2 to 1

Let's say that the shooter has established 4 as the point. If you have $5 bet on the pass-line, you can make an odds bet of $15 at a triple-odds table. If the shooter successfully repeats the 4, you will be paid $5 for the pass-line wager and $30 for the odds bet! Look at the chart. The correct odds of repeating a 4 before rolling a 7 is 2 to 1. That's why your odds bet won $30. The odds bet is just another example of why the game of craps is unique.

There is no other bet in the casino that does not provide a casino advantage!

"Why make such a big deal about a bet that only evens out over a long term?" you might ask. Let me answer your question with my own question. Would you rather make bets that always give the house a rock-solid advantage, or would you prefer a bet that's truly fair? A bet in the casino that doesn't favor the house is a big deal!

THE ODDS BET REDUCES THE OVERALL CASINO ADVANTAGE

Making the odds bet along with the pass-line wager reduces the casino's total pass-line advantage from 1.41 percent to about 0.85 percent. Double odds reduces the house edge even more to about 0.63 percent. Triple odds and ten-times odds and so on can reduce the percentage even more to well under one-half percent! Although the odds bet does not directly affect the house percentage on the pass-line part of the wager, it does lower the percentage for the total amount of your wager. And in reality, that's what you should be concerned about.

The key to using multiple odds bets is in the way you size your bets. Let's compare a pass-line wager of $15 with no odds to another pass-line bet of $5 with $10 in odds. If the point is

10, you would be paid only $15 in winnings for the $15 pass-line wager, compared to $25 for the $5 pass-line bet with $10 in odds. See? It depends on how you structure your bets to earn the advantage of multiple odds without increasing your total risk.

It is worth noting, however, that high multiple odds can be risky. Even triple odds can sting if the dice are not passing (winning). So use common sense in making these bets. Some players use the odds bet as a betting progression of sorts, starting out with double odds and then moving up to triple odds, then four-times odds and so on as long as winnings accumulate. If they lose a bet, they go back down to double odds and start over. It's a betting strategy well worth considering, and one that I strongly recommend you use.

THE COME BET

The **come bet** is best described as a delayed pass-line wager. There's no question where to place it, since the largest block of the table layout is assigned for come bets. The area has COME boldly displayed in the center.

You make come bets while a shooter is rolling for a point. That's the only time you can make a come bet since it's basically just like a pass-line bet. And the same rules apply, which I'm sure you have memorized by now: A 7 or 11 wins on the come; a 2, 3, or 12 loses. Any other number becomes the point number and must be repeated before a 7 rolls in order to win.

Let's say the shooter's point number to win on the pass line has been established as 6. If you wish to have another bet working for you that's just like the pass-line bet, simply place your bet in that section of the come area nearest to your position at the table. Hope for either an 11 or a point number, because a craps will lose your come bet; a 7 will win your come bet, but will lose the pass line.

Now let's say that the next number rolled is a 9. Now you'll be looking for another 9 (before a 7) to win your come bet. It can be said that you have two numbers working: 6 on the line and 9 coming. When a 7 or 11 is rolled while your bet is sitting in the come, the dealer immediately places the payoff directly beside your bet. It is your responsibility to quickly pick up the chips, otherwise the bet works on the next roll as another come bet. However, if a craps is thrown, the dealer simply takes your come bet and it's up to you if you want to make another bet.

If the roll is a 7, the winning come bet is called a **last come**, and is often forgotten by players who make it, especially if that 7 signaled a time to quit. Dealers often yell to players as they exit the table, "Hey, buddy, you forgot your last come!"

THE POINT BOXES

Now you know that come bets are settled in the come for rolls of 7 or 11 or craps. But if the roll is a point number, your come bet does not remain in the come area. The dealer will reposition your bet in the proper box for the point number rolled, and in a spot within that box that's directly referenced to your location at the table. That's the only way that the dealer can keep track of the ownership of bets.

If you're standing along the front of the table, for example, the come bet will be moved to the front of the point box corresponding to your position at the table. If you're standing along the end of the table, your come bet will be moved to the back of the point box. Think of the boxes as having four chip positions along the front for the four potential players along the front of the table, and four chip positions along the back for the four potential players along the end of the table.

Dealers refer to players at a table by their position, placing come bets and place bets in the corresponding position within the point boxes. Dealers, in communication with other dealers, also identify players by this position, such as "2 right" or "3 left" meaning to the right or left of the stick. It's a good idea to keep an eye on your bets in the point boxes. Don't rely on the dealer to keep all the bets straight. Since the come bet is just like the pass-line wager, you can take odds on the come bet too—and you'll definitely want to do that.

HOW TO MAKE AN ODDS
BET FOR A COME BET

To make the all-important odds bet on a come bet that has gone to a point box, simply position the bet (you know the routine) in that section of the come area nearest to your position at the table. That's right—in the same spot where you made your come bet. While doing this, announce to the dealer loudly and clearly, "Odds on my come bet." Otherwise, the dealer might think it's another come bet you're making.

You see, after a point number has rolled, the dealer will already have picked up your come bet and placed it in the point box. It's the first action a dealer takes on rolled point numbers:

He places all come bets in their proper point box location. When the come bet and odds bet are repositioned in the point box, the dealer places your odds bet on top of the come bet, but he offsets it slightly to distinguish the odds bet from the come bet.

When the shooter repeats a come-bet point for you, the dealer will immediately return your come bet and odds bet to the come area where you originally placed them. Next, the dealer will place your winning chips directly beside the bets. Again, if you don't pick up all the chips, they work on the next roll as another come bet. Be careful!

Let me repeat an important aspect of what you've just learned: When you make a come bet and odds bet, always be sure to position the bets in the come area near the perimeter of the come area and in direct line with where you're standing. Don't just throw your chips down or place them anywhere in the come area or your bets may later be confused with another come bet placed by another player. It's your responsibility to keep track of your own bets. There's always some jerk at the tables who thinks your chips are his chips.

WHY MAKE COME BETS?

The best reason I can give you for making come bets with odds, is to gang up on the table when a shooter is repeating a lot of point numbers that would otherwise be useless to you if you were just betting the pass line. Don't let all those beautiful numbers go to waste! That's your cue to make a come bet or two. But, as we talked about in the case of multiple odds, don't go overboard on come bets either.

Like multiple odds, you can use come bets as a form of betting progression. Start out by just betting the pass line. If you win a few bets, make a come bet. If you continue winning, make another. When a shooter's on a roll, I might have as many as three come bets working for me. When one hits, I start another one so that I always have three bets in the boxes. When the inevitable 7 clears the table, I go back to my basic pass-line-only status and wait for another streak of wins before I begin launching come bets again.

OFF AND ON

Let's say you have a come bet on 6, and decide to fire off another come bet so that you can have two come bets in action. You make the bet and the shooter throws your 6. If the come bet you just made and the come bet sitting in the point box are of the same value (not counting odds), the dealer will simply pay your winnings beside the come bet in the come area instead of moving the chips about. Pick up your winnings and let your new come bet stay there awaiting another roll.

If the come bets are not of the same value, it could be confusing to figure out the net winnings. Never let a dealer do this. Insist that the come bet with odds that hit is paid, and the new come bet is moved to the same box awaiting your new odds bet, essentially creating a new bet.

OFF ON THE COME OUT

You can remove your odds bets at any time, or you can simply call them off whenever you like, but there's no particularly good reason for doing it. Of course, you can't remove a pass-line bet or come bet. Otherwise, you would have a healthy advantage by just letting the bets work on the come out roll (where you have a big advantage) and then simply taking the bets down if a point number is established (where the edge swings to the casino). Obviously, the casinos won't go for that! But since the odds bet is fair, no advantage either way, casinos will let you do as you please with it.

However, casinos have a standing rule that all odds bets are automatically off on the come-out rolls unless you say otherwise. The theory is that most players don't want to lose the odds bets in case a 7 is rolled on the come out, which would wipe out all the come bets in the point boxes. In fact, the 7 does wipe out your come bets—but with the odds called "off," the dealer will return all your odds bets to you. It's a standard house rule, so go with it.

PLACE BETS

For the players who are too anxious to get their money on the table, especially on their favorite point numbers, casinos allow bettors to place any or all of the point numbers without having to go through the rigmarole of waiting for them to come up, as a come-bettor must do. But for this luxury, you have to pay a price. Certainly the casino won't pay true odds as it does on your odds bets, no way! Here's a schedule of how the casino pays place bets.

PLACE NUMBER	ODDS PAYOFF	SHOULD BE	CASINO ADVANTAGE
6 & 8	7 to 6	6 to 5	1.52%
5 & 9	7 to 5	3 to 2	4%
4 & 10	9 to 5	2 to 1	6.67%

Placing the 6 or 8 is not a bad bet at all, a meager 1.52 percent house advantage. Occasionally I'll catch myself placing a 6 or 8 if the number is not covered with a come bet. Still, the casino edge is two and a half times greater than a pass-line bet or come bet with double odds. But don't let that stop you if you want to make place bets because the 6 or 8 place bets are the most likely place bets to streak. In the event you do place a 6 or 8, be sure to make your wager in multiples of $6, because the payoff is 7 to 6. For example, if you bet $30 on the 6, the payoff is $35.

Dealers position place bets in the point boxes in a similar fashion to come bets. However, you must tell the dealer what the bet is that you want to make. It's not a big deal; you don't have to carry on a conversation. If you want to bet $6 on the point of 8, simply say, "Six-dollar 8."

ONE-ROLL BETS

There are many popular one-roll bets known as **proposition** or **prop** bets where you either win or lose on the next roll. Perhaps the most popular bet is simply known as **eleven**, also affectionately called "**yo**." The most popular time to bet eleven is on the come-out roll. The house advantage on this wager is a little over 11 percent, which makes it easy to remember, right? Eleven percent for number eleven!

The two other popular one-roll bets are **aces** and **twelve**. There's only one way to make either of these bets: You have to see one dot on each die for aces, and a trainload of dots on the dice for a 12. These two bets torment dice players more than any other. Rarely does a player bet them both; it's usually one or the other. And you know what that means, right? If you bet aces, the train pulls in. If you bet the train, two little dots will laugh in your face. The solution, of course, is to bet them both, but you know what will happen, right? You'll see one die with one dot and the other die with six dots. Well, it's a 7, so at least you won the pass line.

Betting on **any craps** is another one-roll bet that's commonly seen. All the craps numbers—2, 3, and 12—are in play for this 7 to 1 wager. Some players who have worked their pass-line bet up to a significant amount will often make an "any" bet to "insure" their pass-line wagers. But the cost is high: 11 percent.

HARD-TO-RESIST HARDWAYS

Most popular among the proposition bets are **hardways**, but they are not one-roll bets, which probably explains their prevalence among players. As with all the other bets, hardways are simple to make and simple to understand. Here's the gist: The point numbers 4, 6, 8, and 10 are the only ones that can be made in pairs. If a 4 rolls as a pair of 2's, it rolled the **hard way**. If it rolled as 3-1, it rolled **easy**. But winning the bet isn't easy because you lose it when a hardway rolls easy or a 7 clears the table.

As with the other prop bets we've covered, the percentages are steep, though that ominous fact doesn't seem to stop players from loading up on them. Whether they just don't know or just don't care is hard to say, but my best guess is that they *do* know and they *don't* care because they are willing to fight the odds for the bigger payoffs.

Players who know me, or who have read other books I've written about craps, know that I've often related stories about huge wins at the dice tables that resulted from an incredible string of hardway hits. With the higher payoffs for these bets, significant wins can come quickly. When I bet them, however, I treat them as loaded guns. They get all of my respect not only for what they can do when they hit, but for what they can do when they don't hit. They'll eat away at your stake like termites on a log cabin. Accordingly, I only bet them after I've already raided the casino's till. That's right, only when I'm up.

Still, the thrust of this book is to play the percentages, which means finding the low-percentage games and the low-percentage bets. Hardways simply fall short. If you do decide to twirl the cylinders on these bets, do it only when you're up.

ODDS VERSUS PERCENTAGES

A friend of mine called me after he got back from a gambling trip and said he bet twelve hardways during a few hours of play and hit none. "Boy," he said, "you're right about those high-percentage bets!" When I told him that the high percentages had nothing to do with it, it left him in a daze. He never did understand the difference between odds and percentages.

The percentages on those hardways could have been ten times as high and still have nothing to do with his shutout. What difference would it have made what the percentages were? He never got paid on any bets, so there was no percentage working against him. He was simply a victim of the odds, but not to any great extent. He was only going after the hard 6 and hard 8, which roll at true odds of 10 to 1, so in eleven shots, he should have won a hardway, maybe none, maybe two. He took twelve shots; he got none. Big deal.

Remember, anything's possible in the short term, but his term was exceptionally short. Besides, he would have needed to take it into the long term to see the percentages really work (against him). Over the long term, he would have lost by the difference in true odds and paid odds (10 to 1 vs. 9 to 1). An accumulation of short pays would have been his percentage cost. But those twelve trials were hardly a long-term test.

Now you know: You can't always blame the percentages. Sometimes they're not even in the game. Since anything can happen in the short term, you can just about throw the percentages out the window. My friend could very well have called me and said he hit three or four of those hardways (out of twelve shots) instead of hitting none, and that wouldn't have surprised me either. If he had said that he hit all twelve, I would probably have thought he was hitting the sauce too.

Incidentally, the odds expression for prop bets in the center of the layout is defined as **for 1** in some casinos instead of **to 1**, such as "10 for 1" in the case of the 6 or 8 hardways, instead of stating "9 to 1" as most casinos do. Both expressions are the same in terms of winnings—the difference is simply whether your bet stays up or is given back to you with your winnings. Odds of 9 to 1 means that you win 9 times your wager, and your wager stays up. Odds of 10 for 1 means that you are paid 10 times your wager, but your wager is taken down.

Stating the odds as 10 for 1 may lead unsuspecting players to believe they are getting a better payoff. It's a cheap ploy that the casinos should be ashamed of! Both expressions are the same in terms of winnings. The difference is simply whether your bet stays up or is given back to you with your winnings. Odds of 9 to 1 means that you win 9 times your wager and your wager stays up; odds of 10 for 1 means that you are paid 10 times your wager but your wager is taken down.

BET	PAYS	SHOULD PAY	CASINO ADVANTAGE
Hard 6 (or 8)	9 to 1	10 to 1	9.1%
Hard 4 (or 10)	7 to 1	8 to 1	11.1%

Look at the payoffs for hardways and note that the 6 and 8 hardways pay the same, as do the 4 and 10 hardways—but the 6 and 8 hardways pay more than the 4 and 10 hardways and even sport a slightly lower percentage. The reason they pay more is because there are more *easy* ways to make them—in other words, more ways to lose the bet. (Hardways lose when they're made easy.) So, if there are more ways to lose, they should pay more, and they do—6 and 8 hardways pay 9 to 1, and 4 and 10 hardways pay 7 to 1. This is the opposite of what most rookie players expect because they know that the 4 and 10 point numbers are harder to make, so they just expect the 4 and 10 hardways to pay more too. But as I've just explained, they are misguided in their reasoning.

The dealer places hardway bets at the center of the table. Simply toss your bet to the dealer and announce, "Five-dollar hard 6." The bet is placed in a box that, unlike the point number boxes, represents the whole table, not just one end. To find your spot in the box, you first have to mentally divide the box in half. If you're standing beside the dealer just left of center, your spot in the box is the left corner formed by the front edge of the box and that invisible line you drew that divides the box. Don't worry, you'll catch on.

Hardways win when point numbers are made in pairs. If you're on the hard 6, you need a 3-3 to win. Any other 6—1-5, 5-1, 2-4, and 4-2—will lose the bet. Of course, a 7 will also lose the bet. And it doesn't have to be a seven-out. "Hardways work unless called off" is a standard cry of the dice dealers in most casinos. That means you'll lose your hardway bets with a 7 on the come-out roll, unless you call them off.

THE "LADY'S BET"

The **field bet** is a one-roll bet that the next roll of the dice will be a number in the FIELD box—a 2, 3, 4, 9, 10, 11, or 12. There are so many variations on the one-roll field bet today that I can't give you the specific percentages, but let's say around four to five percent. It's a tempting bet to the uninitiated because there are so many field numbers that win—but of course, there are more ways to lose.

It's often called the "lady's bet" because, in the days before women really caught on to craps, all they made were field bets. If a woman asked a craps dealer (all male in those days) for assistance, he would show her the big box on the layout marked FIELD and say, "Put your bet right here, young lady, and if any of those numbers come up, you win." That's craps? No, that's not craps. That was just a brush off.

THE DON'T BETS

The sections of the table layout marked DON'T PASS and DON'T COME are for betting *with* the casino and *against* all the other players, assuming they're not all making **don't bets** (betting the dice will lose). Technically, don't bettors are not betting with the casino, but they do win when the casino wins, except in one case: When a 12 is rolled on the come out, the don't bettor doesn't win; it's a **push** (a standoff). The percentages are about as small as the **right** side (betting the dice will win) and the BAR 12, as the push is called, is worth the 1.40 percent house edge.

The only problem with the don't bets is that you want a cold table in order to win. You win when the other players lose. You're siding with the enemy. I never play the don't side because it's too darn boring. No excitement. And there shouldn't be: It could be dangerous! Don't bettors should never yell and scream and wave their arms when a shooter sevens out. Even though they won, other players might have lost thousands. Winning on the don't with even a smile of arrogance on your face will get you looks that could kill. Be sure a security guard is handy if you plan on touting your win to the other players. If you're the type who likes to antagonize other people, the don't bets were designed just for you.

BEYOND THE BASICS

You positively, absolutely must take the odds on your pass-line and come bets. As you've already learned, the odds bets are the only fair bets in the casino. You cannot ignore them. In fact, you should look for the highest odds you can find. We need to be clear on this. You are not looking for these high-odds tables because you're going to start play at that maximum level right out of the chute. No, that's too risky. The idea is to start with odds that are within your comfort zone, a reasonable multiple. Your plan should be to use the remaining odds available as a progression to work up.

Here's an example. Let's say you start play, as I do, with three red chips on the pass-line ($15), and you are okay with triple odds, as I am. But the table you found offers 10X odds! Win a few hands and work your way up to 5X odds, then 7X perhaps, and finally all the way to ten-times odds! Sure, you'll be putting $150 behind your three chips on the line, but you will have won more than enough, much more, to cover the loss if you lose it. And who's to say you're not going to win it? Think positive going up that ladder.

The proverbial ladder, incidentally, is higher than you think. Even if you hit the 10X odds on the pass line, you probably have some come bets working for you too—I would hope so, if you've stashed away a few pass-line wins—so get those come bets moving up the ladder too.

How you wish to structure your progression is up to you. Just keep the number one goal in mind: To cash in on a hot streak of numbers for all you've got! That's right, pull out all the stops. Strike hard! Those nice, long hot streaks don't happen often; you must learn how to recognize the opportunity early on, and start climbing that mountain of cash.

The secret of taking full odds, or at least working your way up there, is not commonly known to beginning players. But you would think that seasoned players know all about it. Well, apparently not. Recent casino studies have shown that only about 10 percent of players take more than double odds when more is offered. That means that 90 percent of all players are not taking advantage of a key opportunity. Go figure.

I can't end this discussion until we talk about the problems of players who visit regional gambling markets, those with only one or two casinos, and are unable to find 10X odds at the craps tables. They can't find it because there isn't enough competition in these smaller venues to produce better game rules for the players. So, let's say you were only able to find 5X odds. You can still make a mini-progression out of it, starting with double odds and working your way up, one increment at a time, to full odds.

Regardless of the playing conditions you find, always take at least double odds when you begin play. If the casino only offers double odds, I suggest you avoid it and look for something better. By not offering higher multiple odds, these noncompetitive casinos have taken a valuable option away from you. In my home state of Michigan, we have 24 mostly Indian casinos and a bevy of rule variations. When I play there, it's not unusual for me to drive an extra couple of hours to play at a 10X odds table. It's worth it. Today, I won't play craps in a casino that doesn't offer at least 5X odds. I suggest you take the same staunch position.

PLAY THE PERCENTAGES

If you play often, well into the long term, it behooves you to play the percentages. The craps table offers a range of bets from as low as 0.3 percent (the pass-line or come with full odds) to as high as 16.67 percent for a prop bet known as "any 7." If you only play the pass-line and make occasional come bets with triple-or-better odds, you are playing the percentages. So what I'm telling you, I guess, is to forget all the other bets. It's sage advice: You can't play smarter than making only the lowest percentage bets available.

All of the high-percentage bets are these infamous prop bets found at the center of the table layout and in the field. From hardways to one-roll bets chasing down aces or trains (double six), the percentages are at least 9 percent (about half of that for field bets). By the way, the old terms "snake eyes" for aces and "boxcars" for double six have become passé. Using these terms will generally give you away as a rookie player. Avoid these and any of those other slang expressions you might have heard. If you shout, "Baby needs a new pair of shoes!" in reference to the point of 4, today's players will laugh at you.

It is true that I've promoted hardway bets in several of my other writings. My well-known "bomb" strategy for beating craps, which I outlined in *Commando Craps & Blackjack*, is based on hardway betting—but only after you've made significant wins on pass-line and come bets. The concept is to take a small portion of these winnings and "build a bomb" on either the hard 6 or 8. With the 9 to 1 payoff, hitting the hardway (I like to say "explosions") can produce sizable gains and have been instrumental in my major victories. But the smart approach to this game, especially if it's going to run into the long term, is to simply play the percentages—and that means pass-line and come bets with full odds. It's that simple. And yes, it does simplify the game.

There are, however, a couple of place bets—namely, placing the 6 or the 8—that only cost you 1.52 percent. Seems reasonable enough, but it's three times the cost of pass-line bets and come bets with only triple odds. Still, I make exceptions to my rules and you certainly can too. The 6 and 8 place bets are a good example. If I'm riding a nice run of point numbers and have several come bets working, but not on the 6 or 8, I might place these numbers just to have all the bases covered. It's not the smartest move over the long term, but in the short term and under the conditions I just described, who can say?

The 6 and 8 place bets are popular with many players. In fact, there are some players who only play these bets. The payoffs are easy to compute (7 to 6) and they are the easiest to roll among the point numbers. In *Casino Gambling*, I provided these players with a strategy for just these bets. It's never been my intention to chastise players for the way they bet; I certainly don't want to take their fun away. In the case of this unique strategy, called "6 & 8 Power Press," my hope is that it only adds to their fun while providing an important structure to their betting.

START WITH SMALL BETS

Never begin play with relatively large bets, especially multiple bets scattered over the table. Why put yourself in instant jeopardy? Begin with modest bets and increase the size and number of your bets only if wins accumulate. It's a common-sense approach that helps temper the temptation. Simply put, it's too easy—and too tempting—to make too many bets. Remember, start small and build!

Playing with a high-roller friend of mine years ago, I got tired of seeing him get knocked out early time and time again. I had a feeling that he was getting tired of it too, so I told him to play the way I do: Start with three red chips on the pass line and see what happens. Well, let me tell you what happened: Three chips on the line, lost with an ace-deuce. Another three chips, another ace-deuce. Three more chips and then six more behind them as he placed the odds for the point of 4. Three chips in the come, lost with aces.

I stopped him. We watched as a cold dice table finally relented and took him out of his misery with a seven-out. But he wasn't miserable at all. At the coffee shop later, I told him he had just saved about three thousand dollars! "No" he said, "closer to four! I feel like I won!" But he actually won more than that. From that day on, he never again jumped into a game with money flying. To borrow his expression, he would always "test the table with red" before he wrote the big marker. And if he did write a marker, he would always ask for a couple hundred in green chips instead of all black like he used to. The green chips were part of his progression up the color ladder: starting with red, then to green, and hopefully, to black. Stacks of black! With wins stacked behind him.

EXPECT THE UNEXPECTED

At the craps tables, always expect the unexpected. Anything can happen in short-term play! Always be prepared to react to a sudden surge in either direction. Good dice players are focused on the game, keyed to the moment. You don't want to miss out on a nice run of numbers, and you don't want to overstay your welcome either. Craps is a little different from other casino games in the sense that it tends to run in streaks. Since a 7 ends a hand while a shooter is rolling for a point, I guess we can credit those one-in-six odds of rolling that 7 for creating the streaky nature of the game. Although the odds are solid in the long term, they're a little shaky in the short term. That 7 might show up prematurely or it might show up late.

To help you remember this important aspect of the game, look at the previous sentence and find the two words that don't belong. You got it! The words "prematurely" and "late" are clearly inappropriate. Just as there is no such thing as an overdue number or color at the roulette wheel, there are no premature or late 7's at the dice tables. The game is random. You have to expect wild swings in probability, all well within the bounds of mathematical expectation. In other words, when you walk up to a table, learn to expect anything. Anything can happen.

There's no reason to act surprised with a string of quick seven-outs. By the same token, there's little reason to be surprised when the 7 decides to go into hiding. Among all these things that can happen, a nice run of point numbers would be greatly appreciated. A shooter throwing number after number while rolling for his point is what you're looking for. It's fun when the dealer just keeps giving you chips. Another number, more chips—that's what you're looking for. And I hope you find it often.

Every good dice player knows that you can toss out the odds in the short term because anything can happen. Now you know it, too. Keep your play in the short term to increase your chances of winning. Allow me to share with you a short "secret." It's so important that I purposely want to keep it short—and sweet and easy to remember:

The dice tables challenge your discipline more than any other casino game.

I've always believed this is true, so playing in sessions with breaks in between them is one of my own personal disciplines. In fact, short-term sessions are part of my standard casino routine regardless of the game I'm playing. Now don't get me wrong—if I'm winning, I'll stay at the table. I'm not going to close up shop while the dice are dancing. I'm not stupid. As long as I'm winning, I play. But if I walk into an instant cold streak, I will cut the session especially short. And I don't have to see icicles to know that I picked the wrong time. Even if I'm caught up in that typical win-four, lose-five scenario that seasoned dice players call "choppy," I see no reason to keep playing, so I take my break.

I'm not there to *play*—I'm there to *win*! And if I'm not winning, I'm not playing.

POWER PROGRESSIVE STRATEGY

When I started writing about gambling in 1979, one of my first published articles was a thorough whitewashing of the concept of "systems." I debunked even the most complex systems, showing readers how and why they would fail. And over the years, most gaming authors moved away from systems that did little to increase your chances of winning. Not surprisingly, however, many of the older systems that had at least some interesting merit were reprised in the late 1990s, many of them revised versions that are still being circulated to this day. Once again I became intrigued, knowing that we now have a new tool to analyze systems through billions of trials.

Using my analytical experiences of the past and the computer power of today, I've refined these revised systems to more resemble a strategy. How? By closely following the mathematical likelihood of winning progressions. The most powerful of these strategies is what I call "The Power Progressive Strategy," which has many advantages that systems never offered.

It will become quite clear to you that strategies have values in many shapes and sizes. For example, it is my belief that a strategy can work even if it sometimes doesn't produce wins as often as you would like. It may instead help protect you against losses that you would probably incur otherwise. If nothing else, like a good plan, a good strategy gives you an organized, sensible approach to gambling. No more haphazard bets. No more reckless attacks on a game when the conditions say otherwise. There will be reason to your betting, sound reason. Even the most inexperienced of all gamblers will be able to understand the advantages of using a strategy over a system.

INTRODUCTION TO THE POWER PROGRESSIVE STRATEGY

WHO CAN PROFIT FROM THE PPS?

Is The Power Progressive Strategy for everyone? Darn near. Or at least, it should be. The only players we can easily exclude from The Power Progressive Strategy are high rollers. You know, the players who think that the only way they can win big is to bet big, right out of the chute! This dangerous notion is entirely hogwash.

You can win big without betting big!

Winning big without betting big is one of the key principles of The Power Progressive Strategy. The only assurance I can give players who start out with big bets is this—big losses! Maybe not every time, but some time. And for players like you and me, why take that risk? Indeed, the players who take that risk have money trees growing in their backyard. But having big money is certainly no reason to bet big money. If you are so fortunate to have a lot of money and you intend to get your thrills and spills by risking it, you're barking up the wrong tree! And you're reading the wrong book.

TARGET THE PPS FOR EVEN-MONEY WAGERS

The Power Progressive Strategy (PPS) is designed for even-money wagers such as blackjack, the pass-line and come bets at the dice tables, and even roulette.

Although roulette does not sport low enough percentages to be included in this book, it's worth the mention because I know that roulette players will be reading this chapter and hoping they've found a way to reduce the percentages. Of course, no roulette player can really reduce percentages. That is, unless they've found a single zero wheel with either en-prison or surrender offered. And, I might add, with modest betting limits. But some players can reduce the odds against them through judicious betting and structured sessions of attack. The best assault on a roulette wheel is a hit-and-run approach.

There is some question as to whether or not the PPS can be used at the blackjack tables while card counting. Most often, it is used by players who are not counting the cards. I always incorporate both card counting and the PPS when I'm at the blackjack tables. If the count is running in my favor and I'm on a string of wins, I'll push the envelope to the max. After all, I've found not one but both of the game attributes I'm looking for: A positive count of remaining cards, and a streak of winning hands. Can it get any better?

BENEFITS Of THE POWER PROGRESSIVE STRATEGY

As a result of my many years studying the games and particularly the players, it has become clear to me what most players really want from gambling. Obviously, players want to win, but it's how they win that determined the four important traits of the Power Progressive Strategy that make it unique. First and foremost, players want those wins with low risk and high rewards. As any good stockbroker would attest to, winning with low risk and high rewards is first on the list of almost all new investors. And it's exactly what "investors" in the casino want too—token investments, big returns.

Even if they don't want to admit it, most players not only want to win big with little risk, but they also want to win both easily and quickly. It's a sign of the times, I suppose. And it's a tall order. It's why there are fewer players at the racetrack today and more players in casinos. The decisions are faster in the casino—some would say, too fast—and the work factor associated with handicapping is nearly nonexistent in the casino.

My analysis also explains why most patrons in casinos today are slot players. Slots definitely offer low risk and high rewards. Just ask the player who won $5,000 playing a nickel slot! And slot machines are certainly fast, as fast as you can load 'em up, push the buttons or pull the handle. With the exception of certain skill machines such as video poker, there is absolutely nothing to learn, nothing to study, nothing to memorize. Who would argue that slots are easy to play?

All of this also explains why blackjack has become somewhat flat over recent years. New players soon realize that they must bone up on the game to have any chance at winning. Only a few make the decision to work at the game, to really learn it, much as a chess player must do to really appreciate the complexity and strategy of the game. Too many players also pass up the craps tables for much the same reason. The table layout looks complicated, even though the game is gosh-awful easy to play.

Gamblers also shy away from horse racing because they find the action far too, well, slow. Except for those "most exciting two minutes in sports," the rest of the time it's b-o-r-i-n-g, because most new players today have no interest in cracking the *Racing Form* or studying the program. So they wait, and they wait, for the next race. The new wave of racetrack handicappers are not patient. And as you might expect, they are not winners either.

So now we have the components of the Power Progressive Strategy that the younger set finds attractive. It's low risk and high reward; it's quick and easy; and it's fast and furious. But wait, that's only three. There are four: It's fun too. Playing the

PPS has to be fun, otherwise the new wave of players today would shun it. And don't tell me that having fun is automatic when you're playing. Playing isn't fun. Winning is fun!

Gambling isn't fun if you're not in control of your play.

The Power Progressive Strategy helps keep you in control.

Okay, so the PPS is low risk, you have a good chance for a decent win, the pace will keep you on your toes, and the experience is, hopefully, fun. Who could ask for more? Well, I could. And I will. Whenever I play, I must have one driving force always on full power. You might think you know what it is, but I'll lay odds that you don't. It goes beyond that trite expression, the "desire to win." Everyone wants to win. That's no big deal. You see, I've found that desire alone is not going to get the adrenalin pumping. It's not going to keep me on my toes as I continue to play hard in a manner that I call "controlled aggression." Simply defined, that means being aggressive but not stupid.

What works for me is not a reconfirmation of my desire to win; it's so much more than that. Indeed, my driving force is what I call the "anticipation of winning big." That is the force that energizes me on every deal, every roll, every spin, every game, every race. I want to know that I might be only one play away from the biggest score of my lifetime.

But I can't give the casino an ongoing battle. No one can. You need to enjoy that anticipation while at the same time protecting your arsenal of weapons. I call it "staying power," one of my favorite expressions. I create my own staying power, increasing my chances of that big score through judicious play. For those of you who know me, you know exactly what that means. I'm often on the move. I'm not in a hurry, never in a hurry. I'm just moving. A friend of mine says I'm "drawn to the heat." Yeah, I wish. But one thing's for sure: I am an active player.

I like to play in short sessions and take breaks in between. It's a hit-and-run approach to gambling that I particularly like. If the table is good, I'll stay until it turns. If the table is not good, that session will be extra short. I'm often asked why I play this way. "What's the difference," someone will ask me, "if you make your next bet a minute later or 20 minutes later?" It's a big difference! You see, I want to change the time, the window, the rhythm, the frame, the period, the moment, whatever you want to call it. I'm a big believer in timing—we all either time it right or time it wrong. Like you, I'm looking for the right time: I'm searching for opportunities.

Winning is not my motivation—winning is my objective. My motivation is the anticipation of winning and to that end, I want as many shots as I can take! It's like an old-timer told me many years ago, "You've gotta learn how to save your bullets."

For those of you who don't mind betting some of your winnings right back at the casino, the Power Progressive Strategy requires only modest bets at the outset, but calls for some bigger bets as you progress up a winning streak. It is a simple yet effective strategy of reinvesting a portion of your winnings. Please understand that you must be comfortable with your betting. If at any time you're not comfortable with what you're doing, don't do it! With all of its inherent stress, gambling can become insurmountable if you are the least bit uncomfortable with your play.

You must have confidence in what you're doing, tempered with patience and caution.

> Confidence, patience, and caution are the hallmarks of successful players.

THE POWER PROGRESSIVE STRATEGY REVEALED

Now that we've concluded the chapters on craps and blackjack, I believe it would be most helpful to you if I detail the PPS right here since I use it so frequently in the following discussions. Once you learn the basics of this strategy, the concepts of betting will be a breeze for you.

This special strategy can be used for all three of the major table games: craps, blackjack, and roulette. Although I don't cover roulette in this book because of its relatively high percentages, I recognize that thousands of players are using a plethora of strategies for the game, so why not offer the most effective one? If you're a roulette player, remember that the PPS is designed for even-money wagers, so you should only use this strategy for bets such as red/black, odd/even, and high/low.

Now that we're ready to talk about the strategy in detail, it is important that you understand another important set of tenets in the Power Progressive Strategy. The PPS is based on the concept that in any negative-expectation game, the keys to success are:

> 1. Minimizing the number of decisions
> 2. Maximizing the wins in winning decisions
> 3. Minimizing the losses in losing decisions

Playing patiently and taking frequent exits play a big role in our betting strategies, not to mention the very nature of the bets we will be making, such as avoiding the one-roll bets at craps. By practicing these two disciplines, we have already taken a good turn at Key No. 1, minimizing the number of decisions we need to make. All that's left to do is to unleash our winning potential while holding our losses to a minimum.

THE POWER PROGRESSIVE STRATEGY		
	BETS	
PRE-PLAY	$5	
	5	
	5	
RED LEVEL	10	
	15	
	20	
GREEN LEVEL	Repeat Option **25**	
	50	
	75	
BLACK LEVEL	Repeat Option **100**	
	200	
	300	
PURPLE LEVEL	Repeat Option **400**	
	800	
	1,200	
	1,600	
	2,000	

The Power Progressive Strategy combines the advantages of optimum betting (making only the lowest percentage bets) with a mathematically proven, quasi-exponential betting progression. It will help you maximize winnings and minimize losses. It even has built-in rules to help minimize exposure. Whether it keeps you out of the long term, however, is up to you. Only you can decide exactly how attached you want to become to your friendly, neighborhood casino.

As I present The Power Progressive Strategy to you, I'm reminded of what we talked about earlier—that too many players today want "easy" and they want "quick." I can make the strategies easy and, to some extent, quick, but I want you to know right now that "quick" can be a detriment to winning. Players who want to win quickly are the same people who tend to bet recklessly. I'm not going to compromise my strategies just because some players are so wound up with gambling that they need rapid-fire decisions. I want you to learn how to replace your desire for speed with an enjoyment of anticipation.

Of all the places where patience is a virtue, none is a better example than the casino. I honestly don't believe players can win with even a modicum of consistency if they are not patient!

ADVANTAGES OF THE POWER PROGRESSIVE STRATEGY

1. Makes your betting virtually automatic.
   There are no tough decisions to make. Nothing to ponder. You simply let the strategy do the work!
2. Gives you out-of-the-gate protection against sudden losses.
3. Ensures a big payday during a hot streak.
4. Forces you to bet down or quit during a cold streak.
5. Works at all table games.

AN OVERVIEW OF THE POWER PROGRESSIVE STRATEGY

Before we go over the important rules for this strategy, let's talk about how the strategy works. You might think the design looks rather basic, but there's more to it than meets the eye. Note that there are five levels to the progression, beginning with pre-play. Pre-play is your safe harbor. You are not allowed to leave pre-play and enter the progression until you have won three bets in a row. As a further protection, you must quit the session in pre-play if your starting stake of $40 is ever reduced to $20. You will always leave the table with no less than $20.

Once you enter the progression, continue to increase your bet to the next amount listed as you continue to win. If you lose at any time during the run, your next bet—called a "drop-down" bet—will always be three betting amounts lower. If you lose that bet too, it's time to exit the session.

Remember it this way: It takes three wins to get in, two losses to get out.

CHIP COLOR MATCHES BETTING LEVEL		
LEVEL	CHIP	VALUE
Pre-play/Red	Red	$5 Chips
Green	Green	$25 Chips
Black	Black	$100 Chips
Purple	Purple	$500 Chips

Each level will be easy to identify as you play, because your bets will be in the chip color of the levels. In the first level, you'll play with red ($5) chips, just as you will in pre-play, but in the green level, you'll progress to green ($25) chips. In the black level (everyone's favorite!), you'll be betting black ($100) chips—and holding onto your seat. Why? Because the next level, if you get to it, is where the mega-money is. It's the purple level where you'll be betting purple ($500) chips. Technically, the second bet of this level goes to purple, but that's close enough. Some casinos use a different color for their $500 chips, but who cares what color they are as long as there are two nice round zeros after the 5!

Incidentally, if you need to change color as you proceed up the progression, by all means do so. Simply ask the dealer to change your stack of 20 red chips to four green chips, for example. Some dealers tend to pay off bets in the same color, but you want to get new color in your payoffs so that you can have the right color to start the next level. Be sure to use the chip colors correctly as you go up the progression. Using the right chip colors minimizes the number of chips in a bet, makes payoffs easier, and helps you know exactly where you are in the progression.

THE POWER PROGRESSIVE STRATEGY'S TRANSITION BETS	
	$5
	$5
	$5
Transition Bet	**$10**
	$15
	$20
Transition Bet	**$25**
	$50
	$75
Transition Bet	**$100**
	$200
	$300
Transition Bet	**$400**
	$800
	$1,200
	$1,600
	$2,000

An interesting design element of this new progression can be noted with each **transition bet**, the first bet of a new level. Note that this wager is only one unit higher than the previous level and, in a sense, follows the previous level's progression. This transition bet was carefully designed into the strategy to help ease you along to the next level while extending the diminishing percentage of increase within a four-bet run (10, 15, 20, 25, for example).

POWER PROGRESSIVE STRATEGY RULES

The progression *per se* is only a part of the strategy. It will not work for you if you don't adhere to the strategy rules. Following the rules is just as important as following the progression!

1.	Take a $40 stake to the session.
2.	Enter the session with a pre-play bet of $5.
3.	Exit the session if:
(a)	you lose two bets in a row, or
(b)	your stake drops to $20.
	See my notes for craps players at the end of this list.
4.	Enter the progression only after you win three bets in a row.
5.	Increase your bet to the next betting amount shown in the progression as long as you continue to win each bet.
6.	Decrease your bet by three betting amounts following a loss in the progression. This decreased bet is called a drop-down bet.
7.	If the drop-down bet wins, continue the progression from that point.
	If the drop-down bet loses, you must exit the session subject to Rule 3a.
8.	If you make multiple bets, treat each bet independently

A SPECIAL NOTE FOR CRAPS PLAYERS REGARDING RULE 3:

If you are making multiple craps bets, a loss on one bet followed by a loss on another bet is *not* two losses in a row. Rule 3a applies to each wager. These losses, however, are subject to rule 3b (aggregate wagers).

Rule 3a seems too stringent to some readers, but the reasons behind this rule are solid: more breaks and less exposure to negative trends.

At blackjack, a split or double down is considered one play. There are no "double" wins or losses. If you split and win one hand and lose the other, it is a "no play."

POWER PROGRESSIVE STRATEGY RULES IN DETAIL

1. TAKE A $40 STAKE TO THE SESSION

Learn how to start each session with the same-size stake. All good gamblers I know do this. It's a mark of discipline. Don't walk up to a table and fish around in your pockets for whatever you can scrounge up—it just doesn't look professional. Have two twenties ($40) ready to go. Exchange them for chips by setting the bills on the table directly in front of you (but not within a betting area) while saying loud and clear, "Change forty dollars, all red chips please."

When I do this at a dice table where the whole table is a betting area, I purposely lay the bills across part of the field and part of the come, two adjacent betting areas within easy reach of the dealer. That way, in case I'm confronted with a deaf dealer, there's no question that my money doesn't play. Ultra-conservative players might be concerned about starting out with $40. They shouldn't be: $40 is not a loss-limit. On the contrary, Rule 3b limits your loss for the session to $20.

So why not start out with $20 instead of $40? Because I also want you to learn how to leave a cold table with a goodly portion of your stake. It may only be psychological, since either way it's a $20 smack in the teeth, but I never want to put you in a position where you walk away with nothing. There's no worse feeling! Incidentally, just because Rule 3a says you walk at $20, that doesn't mean you can't walk earlier. That's something else I don't want to do—I never want to come across as forcing you to play to a certain limit or for a certain length of time. Quit whenever you want to.

After exiting a session, go directly to the cage and exchange the remaining chips for cash. And if you're like me, you'll record the session in your journal. Doing these things has a secondary purpose: It gives you something to do during your break from the tables. You might even want to get a cup of coffee and plan your next session. Whatever you decide, let patience guide you. I don't want to see you in a rush to get back to the tables.

This is an important discipline to follow so allow me to repeat it: Always cash in your chips when you exit a session. Never begin a session with chips. Always begin a session the same way: with cash, two twenties. If you have won a considerable amount of money from prior sessions, lock up your money. Literally. Never carry large amounts of cash on your person. Most casinos offer safety deposit boxes at no charge to you. Another advantage of using a safety deposit box is to keep you away from your winnings. I hate to see players risking more than just a small portion of their winnings for stake money.

Key question: So when do you go back and tackle the table again? Is five minutes too soon? You're darn right it is! Take a break. Relax, eat lunch, take a walk. Check out some other tables. Check out the pool. Check out the action (at the tables, that is). What's the point of quitting a bad table if you're going to head right back?

2. ENTER THE SESSION WITH A PRE-PLAY BET OF $5

Pre-play starts with $5—and you'll stay at that betting level until you can string three wins together. Since this strategy will be used only for bets with even-money payoffs, which usually have decent percentages, you'll encounter that typical win-one, lose-one scenario often. There is little movement in terms of wins or losses, so the $5 betting limit is not going to be much of an issue. No one would say, "Gee, I wish I were betting $25 instead." Breaking even is breaking even.

If you find yourself winning only one bet out of three— which isn't that unusual either—you will be thankful that you are restricted to your $5 limit. On the other hand, if the table conditions look promising and you've managed to win three out of three, what better indicator to start moving up a little?

When I mention pre-play to some of my friends who bet much more heavily than I do, I get quite a laugh.

"Five bucks? You've got to be kidding!"

Funny, isn't it? You don't even have to be a high roller to look down your nose at a five-dollar bill. For the high rollers of the world, $5 isn't even good enough for tip money. And it certainly won't get them any comps. Too bad! This book is for players who want to win money, not comps. It's for players who bet to win, not to impress.

Let's get serious for a moment. Remember that this rule is for openers, what I call "early betting." Judging the potential of the strategy by the $5 pre-play bet is like watching a quarterback on the opening drive, and then deciding whether or not he's going to carry his team to victory. There's so much of the game left to play. It's how the game ends up hours later that counts. Sure, you might have seen him fumble on that opening drive, but now he's piling up the points. It's the same thing at the tables. You might start out slowly, but later on you might creep up the progression and run into some decent-sized bets. You might even reach the high roller level. Trouble is, most of those guys like to start with the big bets. And guess what usually happens?

If you saw me playing at the beginning of a session, you might be surprised and perhaps bored watching me bet a thin nickel at the dice table with an even thinner dime for odds. Five dollars on the pass-line and ten bucks in odds is not going to pop many eyes. No jaws are going to drop. But I'm not bored, and I really don't care what anyone else thinks about the way I play. I know what I'm doing. I'm busy. I'm hunting. Like most players, I'm after the hot shoot that can send me up the progression. Unlike most players, however, I bide my time in getting there, if I get there. Either way, I enjoy the hunt.

Now, if you were to see me again at that same table a half-hour or so later, it's possible that I might be throwing black chips around like candy. I might have a couple thousand in chips spread over the table with piles more in front of me. You might actually confuse me with a high roller (what an insult!). That's what the Power Progressive Strategy can do for you.

3. EXIT THE SESSION IF YOU LOSE TWO BETS IN A ROW, OR IF YOUR STAKE DROPS TO $20.

This important rule protects you against the possibility of getting beaten by a negative streak. By limiting the streak to two, we've nipped it in the bud. We're looking for hot streaks, not cold streaks, so it's time to search elsewhere. Why take the chance that these cold streaks will only continue? Understand that the lose-two-in-a-row-and-you're-out rule applies at any time—in pre-play or while riding the progression, as Rule #7 also makes clear.

Always keep an eye on your stake. Don't ignore the importance of rule #3b. If your stake ever drops to $20, it's quitting time. It might mean a short session, but who cares? You've escaped! You've salvaged half your stake to start a new one. There's always a new session to look forward to, right? Don't think that rule #3b is too strict. It isn't. The critical exit rule is simply to guard against an indiscernible trend. Dice players call this condition "choppy." What it really means is that the game is beating you so slowly that you don't realize it. Stop the trend at $20.

Incidentally, don't be concerned that you're exiting sessions too frequently as you apply rule #3. You'll definitely find that there are more times than you imagined when the rules tell you to quit. And what you'll be doing is something you probably never did as often as you should have—restricting your losses! But that's not all. As you can appreciate, the best time to restrict your exposure is when you're losing.

Restrict your losses. Restrict your exposure. Two for the price of one!

4 & 5. ENTER THE PROGRESSION AFTER YOU WIN THREE BETS IN A ROW, AND INCREASE YOUR BETS FOR AS LONG AS YOU CONTINUE TO WIN EACH BET

This is the fun part! You've won your three-nickel bets, you've paid your dues, and now you're ready to get strapped in and ride the progression. You'll want to take it as far as it will let you.

As long as you win, proceed to the next betting amount. Just let it happen. Don't be nervous. You'll have plenty of protection from previous wins. There are only three places in the progression where a loss might be less opportune than others. Those spots are where the bets press, as marked with a notation on the chart that says "Repeat -Option." It means exactly what you think: You have the option of repeating the bet before the press. The theory is that winning the repeat option makes you better prepared to lose the press. I don't make repeat options anymore, but you can. It's entirely up to you.

Incidentally, readers sometimes tell me how high up the progression they've gone. As you can appreciate, most of the time the progression takes you only into the red level. The thinking for most new players is that making it to the green level is just average. No, getting to the green level is good. Darn good!

Getting to the purple level is a great goal to shoot for, but we must be realistic: Reaching it is on a par with hitting 8 out of 8 on a keno ticket. Okay, that's not quite true but the point is clear. Making it to the purple level is an incredible feat.

6. DECREASE YOUR BET BY THREE BETTING AMOUNTS FOLLOWING A LOSS IN THE PROGRESSION

Yes, all good things do come to an end at some point. This rule protects you from doing something stupid like continuing the progression after a loss. "Never press a loss" is an old gambling maxim that certainly applies here. "**Press**" means to double the amount of your previous wager in the hope of both winning the bet and making up for the loss.

Indeed the correct move is to reduce your bet with a drop-down wager—and that's what Rule #6 tells you to do. Your next bet following a loss in the progression is reduced in proportion to the size of your losing wager. Simply drop down three betting amounts and that's your new starting point. If you are in the red level, your drop-down bet will be in pre-play, which means you need to follow pre-play rules and win three out of three bets before you can get out again.

Some players elect to exit the session after a losing bet that has ended a lengthy progression. Let's say they were at $100 when they lost the bet. They can't bring themselves to cut back, especially all the way down to a lowly $25, so they quit. They had the thrill of betting black chips, not to mention the thrill of a nice win streak, and they figure they'll be able to appreciate the value of that $25 chip after taking a break and then starting up again with a nickel on the line. And they are so right: Values diminish as you go back down. After all, you've been there. But going up, you're heading where you probably haven't been, which means those betting levels are a new and tasty experience.

After a loss, certainly you can quit if you like. Quitting is far superior to continuing the progression, but the smarter choice is to follow Rule #6 and simply cut back by three betting amounts. With all the success you've just had, it's possible that the loss was just a blip in your immediate future—and you might be headed right back up again.

7. IF THE DROP-DOWN BET WINS, CONTINUE THE PROGRESSION FROM THAT POINT, BUT IF IT LOSES, EXIT

This interesting rule covers both situations following a drop-down bet. Losing the drop-down wager means that you've lost two bets in a row and you just heard the factory whistle. It's quitting time, no options, no whining: You exit the session. Your first losing bet was your biggest bet. Your second losing bet was probably also big, relatively speaking. It would be pure stupidity to risk losing another one.

If you win the drop-down bet while in the progression, continue with the progression at the next amount directly higher than the drop-down bet. For example, if your first loss was $100, your drop-down bet will be $25. If you win that bet, your next wager will be $50. If you lose the $50 bet, your drop-down wager will be $15. Losses take you down; wins take you up. That's the gist of the Power Progressive Strategy. Makes sense, doesn't it? It should make all the sense in the world to you.

Losses take you down; wins take you up.

There's something else you should know before we go on to the last rule. We talked about it while discussing Rule #6 and now we'll repeat it: Nothing says you can't quit instead of returning to pre-play or making a drop-down bet. If you want to quit, quit! In fact, quit any time you want to, although I can't understand why anyone would want to quit while riding a nice win streak. Most often, when players elect to quit on their own (not being forced to quit by rule), it's usually when they otherwise would have been relegated to pre-play. But if you feel like playing some more, follow the pre-play rules and see if you can re-enter the progression. If pre-play doesn't work out and you're forced to exit the session, go outside and get some fresh air. It's probably time for a break anyhow.

8. IF YOU MAKE MULTIPLE BETS, TREAT EACH BET INDEPENDENTLY

If you decide to make multiple bets, common at the roulette and dice tables, you must learn how to keep track of these bets as they relate to all the rules. Why? Because each bet is a separate bet independent of other bets, and is subject to all the rules we've just gone over. However, all bets are considered combined for the important Rule #3b.

It's not unlikely that you might have one bet riding a progression while another bet or two are resting in pre-play. When you're in the progression, it's easy to tell where you are by simply looking at the size of your wager. In pre-play, however, you need to remember where you stand with the three-out-of-three rule. Keeping track of one bet is easy. Keeping track of two bets is also easy. But three bets might take a little doing. Some players I know use a scratch pad. Others keep track by stacking chips in front of them. However you do it, don't release a bet into the progression until it has earned its way.

BETTING TARGETS

The Power Progressive Strategy is based on a table-minimum wager of $5. But what if you can't find a $5 table? What if you're reading this book many years after I penned it and the effects of inflation have taken their toll? We all know about inflation, right? In the casino, it means the table minimums go up but the valet who parks your car still gets the same dollar tip.

Even if you're reading this book in its first printing, you still might have trouble finding a $5 table, especially on holidays and weekends. On Friday night the tables are all $10 minimum. On Mondays and all the other weekdays, those same tables are $5. It's all too easy for me to say, "Don't play on holidays or weekends." Some players have no other choice. You also might have trouble finding a low table minimum if you play in a market where there is little or no gaming competition. Some one- or two-casino markets have high table minimums every day! And you thought only players were greedy? Guess again. I have answers to a lot of your gambling problems, but I have no answer for this one. I deplore the concept of setting high table minimums. I hate any tactic where the casino is plainly taking advantage of its huge supply of customers. What's worse, I know that most of you will fall for the casino's ploy. Why? Because you want to play. But higher table minimums will have a chilling effect on the way you play. Right off the bat you're being pushed, you're being forced into doing something you don't want to do. And you'll find yourself in a foul mood because of it. I can't think of a worse way to begin gambling.

I urge you to look for casinos that have reasonable table minimums. Outside of Nevada, that probably means trying your darndest to play on a weekday. It is possible to alter the Power Progressive Strategy, but it's a compromise I don't like. An example would be to start pre-play at $10 (assuming a $10-minimum table) and simply start the red level at $15. A key concept of The Power Progressive Strategy is to restrict your initial bets to minimum levels until you start winning. If these initial bets are substantial due to high table minimums, the casino has just defeated your strategy. Don't give them the opportunity!

5 ATTACKING VIDEO POKER

Are you one of the multitudes of casino players searching for a low-percentage game but you're a bit apprehensive about table games? Here's your answer: video poker! I knew several of the original inventors and designers of the video poker machine, a somewhat radical departure from the traditional slot machine. Even while the new machine was still on the drawing board, they were confident that they had a winner.

Video poker introduced an element of skill to playing a slot machine. Players could make choices—intelligent choices, hopefully—to improve their winning chances. No zombie-like actions just pulling a handle, crossing your fingers or closing your eyes, and hoping for a jangle of electronic bells and buzzers to indicate a win. Maybe not a big win, but something to cause coins to drop into your tray and produce that lovely clinking sound that gives you a chance to show off to your neighbor players. The sound of coins dropping into a tray is a thing of the past of course, except for those rare moments when you push the cash-out button on an electronic machine, but even then there is little clinking. The point is that, whether electronic or honest-to-goodness coin clinking, back in those days there just wasn't anything a machine player could do to get his machine to make noise more frequently.

The guys who put video poker on the market so many years ago were very familiar with this scenario. They suspected that slot players were getting tired of having to rely solely on luck to beat slot machines, so they concocted video poker as an answer to the problem. The Gaming Control Board gave them a "go for launch" in 1976 when hundreds of machines hit the Nevada markets. There was only one problem: No clinking. Not from these rogue machines anyhow, machines that apparently looked too complicated to play. But more than that, they didn't look like a slot machine at all! Slot players, especially in the old days, were a fickle bunch. They actually liked the idea that luck was the determining factor, the only factor, in whether they won or lost. They didn't want to do any thinking, heaven forbid, and they scoffed at the notion that relying on luck was in some way just a slot player's misfortune.

"You think luck doesn't play a role at the table games? Luck is part of all the games!" was one of the many responses from surveys conducted after video poker machines laid the biggest bomb in slot history. The video poker design team did its job—the marketing and research team apparently didn't do theirs. It would be nearly ten years before video poker would finally catch on.

The slot industry experts today believe it took that long simply to change players' attitudes about winning and losing, particularly the attitudes of "senior" players, as the industry calls the over-50 gang. But what really brought the game into widespread acceptance was younger players. They were more technology savvy and more apt to investigate an intriguing new offering. They liked the idea that an element of skill was incorporated into the design. Sadly, though, many players didn't use the skill advantage available to them; they didn't develop the skill to lower the percentages. Even today, I see players who have no earthly clue which cards to hold and which ones to toss.

HOW TO PLAY THE GAME

Before we get into the winning secrets of this great game, let's go over the rules and learn the basics. Video poker is basically five-card draw poker. It is played in much the same way as the live game except that you are paid solely for the value of your hand—you don't have to bet your cards against other players, so there's no bluffing and raising and calling and folding and all that sort of thing. There are no other players to try and outfox to make a weak hand beat a stronger hand, as you might do at the games in the casinos' poker rooms.

Video poker is you against a machine. That's all. And that's the reason many players like it. No intimidation. No pressure. No psychological skills to learn. After all, how could you out-psych a machine? Just as a dealer at the live game delivers five cards to each player, the machine game begins the same way. The machine delivers five cards to you on your screen after you have hit the **deal/draw** button. Then you have a decision to make: You can keep as many cards as you like to make the best poker hand. You can keep one, two, three, four, or all five cards—or you can decide not to keep any of them. You indicate the cards you want to hold by pushing the **hold** button below each card on the screen.

Note to new players: Make sure the machine has registered your hold of a particular card by displaying the word "hold" on the screen above the card you held. Sometimes a machine will not register a card you held, even though you pushed the button. If that happens, and you then push the deal/draw button, it will replace the card you thought you held. Careful players catch machine errors such as this, but those who play too fast often miss the malfunction. All casinos have a standard rule that machine malfunctions are up to the players to catch. You should also report the problem to a floor supervisor.

Now it's time to see if you can improve your hand. Push the deal/draw button again and the machine will remove the cards you didn't hold and replace them with new cards. At this point, the machine will let you know if you've made a winning hand by highlighting on the screen the winning hand you've made and paying you for it based on the paytable displayed on the screen.

If you made three-of-a-kind (three cards all of the same value, such as three kings), you'll be paid three times the amount of your wager. However, note that the paytables tell you how much you will *collect*, not how much you've actually won, as your bet is included in the amount you collect. In our example, you really have won only two times your bet since you have to subtract your bet from the amount you collect. Therefore, your net win for three-of-a-kind is two times your wager: You were paid 2 to 1.

Since the whole idea is to make the best poker hands, obviously it is essential that you know the rank of hands. Here's a chart to help you.

RANK OF JACKS-OR-BETTER POKER HANDS

In descending order, here is the ranking of poker hands for jacks-or-better video poker machines with no wild cards. After a few hours of play, the rank of hands will become second nature to you.

Royal Flush: Any Ace-King-Queen-Jack-10 of the same suit (spades, hearts, diamonds, or clubs).

Straight Flush: Any five cards in consecutive value and of the same suit, such as the 6-5-4-3-2 of diamonds.

Four-of-a-Kind: Any four cards of the same value, such as 8-8-8-8.

Full House: Five cards that include a pair and a three-of-a-kind, such as a pair of kings and three jacks.

Flush: Any five cards of the same suit, such as the A-Q-10-8-4 of hearts.

Straight: Any five cards in consecutive value but not of the same suit, such as 8 of clubs, 7 of hearts, 6 and 5 of spades, and 4 of diamonds.

Three-of-a-Kind: Any three cards of the same value, such as three queens.

Two Pairs: Two pairs of equal-value cards, such as two jacks and two tens.

Jacks-or-Better: Any pair of jacks, queens, kings, or aces.

BEYOND THE BASICS

Video poker is the only slot machine game where you can shop for the best percentages. Why? Because the paytables are not all alike—there are well over a hundred different paytables, although only a dozen or so are frequently found in today's casinos. Clearly it is important that you learn to recognize and compare the different paytables. Most often, the determining factor in whether or not a machine's paytable is low-percentage is the payout for a full house, a flush, and two pair. Based on a one-coin payout, the machine to look for pays nine coins for a full house and six coins for a flush. Two coins are paid for two pair.

Look for this optimum paytable on jacks-or-better video poker machines:

| JACKS-OR-BETTER OPTIMAL PAYTABLE ||
HAND	PAYOUT
Royal flush	250
Straight flush	50
4 of a kind	25
Full house	9
Flush	6
Straight	4
3 of a kind	3
Two pair	2
Jacks or better	1

On all payouts except the royal flush, the payouts for multiple coins are linear; that is, if the one-coin payout is 6, the five-coin payout is 30. So if you're looking at a 9-6 paytable showing the payouts for five coins inserted, the payouts for a full house and a flush will be 45 and 30 coins respectively.

Note that the jacks-or-better machines you're most likely to find today, including those in major gaming markets, are called 8-5 machines (eight coins for a full house and five coins for a flush). When played with optimum skill, the percentage on these games is about 3 percent. In noncompetitive markets, it's not unusual to find 6-5 machines (only six coins for a full house and five coins for a flush). The percentage is a little over 5 percent, so you might as well settle in at a roulette wheel and take your lumps. Clearly you must avoid the 8-5 and 6-5 machines, playing only machines with 9-6 paytables. I hope you can find them.

One thing is for sure: The better paytables are on the higher-priced machines. You won't find a 9-6 nickel machine, and it's even tough to find a 9-6 paytable on a quarter machine in noncompetitive markets. Fifty-cent and dollar machines should give you the best percentages, but look at the paytables to be sure. If they don't, the casino you're in does not deserve the pleasure of your money.

BONUS FEATURES

Many of today's jacks-or-better types of machines offer bonus features. There are several popular variations: bonus poker, double bonus poker, double double bonus, bonus deluxe, and so on. All of them have one thing in common: They award additional jackpots at the expense of smaller wins, usually for two pair. That's right: Two pair is paid the same amount as jacks-or-better.

The bonus machines do have their come-ons, however. In addition to the standard royal-flush jackpot, you might find a bonus jackpot for a sequenced royal (A-K-Q-J-10 in order), or maybe a specifically suited royal flush pays a higher jackpot. In some cases, the payouts for four-of-kind, which is 125 coins for five coins inserted on a standard jacks-or-better machine, are different depending on the rank of the four-of-a-kind. For example, on double-bonus poker machines, four 2's, 3's, and 4's pay 400 coins; four 5's through kings pay 250 coins; and four aces pay a whopping 800 coins.

It looks good, but the cost of not getting paid your even-money win for two pair is more significant than most players think. It's all based on frequency. How many times would you expect to make two pair; how many times would you expect to make four aces? What's more, most of these bonus machines are based on 8-5 paytables! Just exactly how good are these bonus machines? It turned out that they were not as good as players originally thought. Big surprise!

As a response to this growing concern among video poker players, the manufacturers have now designed better bonus machines that take the edge off of the short pay for two-pair by bumping up the payoff for a flush to seven coins and offering the standard machine's top full-house payoff of nine coins. This is a bonus 9-7 machine that is well worth the effort to find. And guess what? Now the manufacturers are offering 10-7 machines in the standard configuration with the bonus features for four-of-a-kind. We're talking percentages here that rival the best bets at a craps table, on the order of only a few tenths of a percent.

These top-rated machines, however, are still in the minority. They are hard to find. The bulk of what you will find are 8-5 bonus and a few 9-6 standard jacks-or-better machines. So remember, most of the bonus machines today give you something extra but take something away. It can't come as any surprise that what it takes away is worth more than what it gives you.

It would seem that the only complicated part of video poker is determining percentages. If all the machines were the same, the percentages would be the same and everyone would be happy, right? Hardly. You know as well as I do that if there were no variations in percentages, the casino industry would settle for a piece of the pie that would be far too expensive for us. That's right: The casinos would gorge themselves. We should look at the variations in percentages as a plus, a competitive element that keeps the overall playing conditions rather decent.

STRATEGY FOR VIDEO POKER SESSIONS

For those of you who still look at percentages with a bit of skepticism, here's something else you can do that will show a machine's true colors. A few years ago, I wrote a series of articles on game percentages and then published these articles in a book titled *How To Win!* The idea was well received by slot players and even today, I still see players practicing the strategy.

The concept is simple, so let me give you an idea of what it's about.

Every time you sit down to play, start with a particular denomination bill (I usually start with $20) and make sure you know the total number of plays at maximum coins that the bill will give you. With my twenty-dollar bill, for example, I know that I have 80 quarters at five quarters per play. That's 16 plays I can expect from my buy-in, so I play the machine 16 times. At the end of that run, I take a count of the credits on the meter. If I have more than 80 credits, the machine has given me a positive expectancy. If I have fewer than 80 credits, I was the victim of a negative expectancy. Over the long term, the machine is built on a negative expectancy, so I must keep a careful watch of the results for every 80 coins I play.

I think of my play in terms of twenty-dollar sessions but, unlike at the table games, I may very well run one session right after another, and keep running until the machine refuses to cooperate. Then it's break time while I plan for my next session at a different machine. It is arguable whether or not this tactic will lead you to more positive sessions than negative, but it does do one thing: It allows you to monitor a machine's percentages at the most important time—the time during which you're playing it!

Regardless of the paytables you find, you should play all five coins each and every time you play a game. It's called "play the max" and it ensures that you are in the running to win the bonus royal flush jackpot with maximum coins in play. All payouts on a video poker machine are linear (wins increase in direct proportion to the number of coins inserted)—except for the royal flush jackpot, which is *not* linear. It is at least 16 times more than the one-coin payout (250 coins) for making a royal. So instead of winning 1,250 coins for five coins inserted, you'll win 4,000! And it could be considerably more if you're playing a progressive machine.

If playing five coins is too steep for you, drop down in coin value. Just as you would move up in coin value as you continue to win, simply drop down when you need to in order to be comfortable with five coins inserted. If you can only afford to play five coins on a nickel video poker machine, however, be advised that you will not find attractive paytables, as the best ones begin with quarters. Hopefully, quarter machines are a good starting point for you as you rack up wins and begin moving up the coin denomination ladder. It's an easy betting progression for slot players that I particularly like. But if you've moved up to a dollar machine and wins aren't coming in the numbers you were finding at the quarter or fifty-cent machines, drop back down in a hurry. Otherwise, you might give back your winnings in a fraction of the time it took to win them. Let common sense prevail.

STRATEGY FOR DRAWING CARDS

There are certain strategies to follow in which cards to hold—that is, what hands to draw to—that make playing the game as routine as using Basic Strategy at the blackjack tables. Best of all, there is one particular strategy that takes into account all of the variations in paytables. If you thought that playing video poker in the most optimum fashion was difficult, you're wrong. It's not complicated, it's fun—and armed with a powerful strategy, it can be profitable too.

Many video poker strategies on the market today are far too conservative to result in significant short-term wins, particularly of the higher jackpots. To make sense of all this, taking the paytable variations into account and presenting the ideal strategy for all players (called a hybrid strategy), I've published a Strategy Card on video poker that covers just about everything. It not only shows the rank of hands and the optimum paytable most likely to be found, but also the best strategy to play for those of you who want to win the bigger jackpots more frequently. For example, it is designed to increase your chances of hitting a royal flush by 20 percent.

For those of you who are thinking that you have to buy something to get the strategy, you don't. Ladies and gentlemen and children of all ages (18 or over in most Indian casinos), step right up and feast your eyes on the best video poker strategy in all the world—I've always wanted to say that!

VIDEO POKER DRAW STRATEGY	
Start at the top of the chart and work down until you find your hand. Stand on straights or better, except for a straight flush that includes four cards to a royal flush.	
YOU HAVE	**DRAW**
4 OF A ROYAL	1
3 OF A KIND	2
4 OF ST FLUSH	1
3 OF A ROYAL	2
2 PAIR	1
HIGH PAIR	3
4 OF A FLUSH	1
OE STRAIGHT	1
2 OF A ROYAL	3
LOW PAIR	3
CL STRAIGHT	1
3 OF ST FLUSH	2
1 HIGH CARD	4
DEFINITIONS: HIGH PAIR: Jacks, Queens, Kings, Aces LOW PAIR: 2's thru 10's OPEN-END STRAIGHT (OE): Four consecutive cards (excluding an ace) CLOSED STRAIGHT (CL): An inside card is missing (8-7-5-4, for example)	

Like other reel-type slot machines, video poker machines can often be found in what are known as **progressive banks** where the machines are electronically tied together so that the more play the machines get, the higher the royal flush jackpot grows. It's possible that the jackpot could increase to a point where the overall percentages actually swing to the players' favor! Some progressive machines also have **add-on jackpots**, such as increased payouts for four aces, straight flushes, and so on. Just as the paytables can vary on stand-alone machines, so can the jackpots and paytables on progressive machines.

Although most video-poker jacks-or-better progressives use 8-5 machines, you can still get the edge if the royal flush jackpot exceeds a certain level. Let's assume you're playing an 8-5 quarter machine where a 4,000-coin jackpot correlates to a $1,000 win. The percentage against you on the 8-5 is higher than the 9-6 because of the short payouts for the full house and flush. But let's say you've found an 8-5 quarter progressive machine and the meter above the carousel reads $1,500. Such a significant increase in your jackpot potential eats away some of that percentage against you.

The only way you can beat the machine with a fair modicum of consistency, however, is by landing the royal. If you don't get the royal, chances are the machine will take a chunk of your money no differently from what a standard machine would do over the long term. That's why you must make your draw decisions without error. And you must play with a bankroll that can survive the ups and downs of such a valiant try. Although there are differing opinions on how large the jackpot has to be to swing the edge in your favor on a bank of 8-5 jacks-or-better progressive machines, I like to use the 120 percent rider as a basis for determining whether or not I want to tackle it. A 120 percent rider means the jackpot should be $2,200 on an 8-5 quarter progressive carousel. That puts us slightly ahead of the game, on paper, and we'll just have to see if we have the stamina to see it through.

The downside to this strategy is obvious. Just because the jackpot is so high, and just because you can play the hands perfectly—and even if you have an unlimited bankroll—there certainly cannot be a guarantee that you'll hit the royal. If for no other reason, some other player might hit it before you do! Hey, that's the chance you take. Worse yet, the likelihood is slim that you'll even find an open machine to play when the progressive jackpot is very high. Years ago, casinos that offered progressive video poker carousels with 8-5 machines were bombarded with professional teams that took over all the machines when the progressive meter topped two grand. They would march in at 4 a.m., when the machines were usually sitting idle, and take them over, literally holding the machines captive. The casino's regular customers complained, and many casinos reacted by establishing stringent rules about team play. Still, it goes on and some players do make out like bandits.

Believe it or not, slot players need to be concerned with money management more so than table-game players. Why? Because of the speed of the machine games. But whether you're a slot player or a blackjack player, having a set of basic disciplines is crucial to your success. In a sense, it's a strategy. Basic discipline and plain common sense are perhaps the most important strategies of all!

Here are a few choice pieces of advice to help you start putting your own rules and regulations together. Carry them with you every time you visit the casino and read them before you play. Casinos have their own rules that they follow to the letter. Professional players strictly adhere to their own unique set of rules. Casual players need their own rules too. Win or lose, you'll feel better about yourself if you know that you played by your rules.

THE SMART PLAYER'S STRATEGY: 12 RULES
1. MAKE SURE YOUR BANKROLL FITS THE GAME
Don't be underfinanced, but don't be overfinanced either. Both of the extremes can be a problem. My advice is to find your comfort level and stick with that same bankroll amount for all of your gambling trips. If your trips vary in length, assign

a certain stake per day. The key here is continuity. Drastic variations in your bankroll can have a negative effect on the way you play.

2. DO NOT RUSH TO PLAY

Upon arrival at the casino, be prepared with something else to do first. Temper your anxiety. It might be something as simple as having breakfast or lunch, or meeting friends over coffee. Maybe you've had a long flight or a long drive. It's absolutely essential that you change gears, relax, and get in the right frame of mind before you challenge the machines.

3. OBSERVE BEFORE YOU PLAY

A lot can be gained by simply watching, particularly if you're thinking about playing a certain bank of machines. Watch the other players. Although you can't be assured that all the machines sport the same percentages, you might discover from watching others play that more walking is in order. At the very least, judicious observing helps you by minimizing your exposure.

4. ALWAYS PLAY THE MAXIMUM NUMBER OF COINS

I've given you all the reasons why you should play maximum coins; I can only hope I have convinced you. Obviously, our play-the-max rule only applies to 5-coin machines. Watch out for the new arcade-style 10-coin machines or the new triple-play machines that are really three machines in one. Players tell me these machines are hard to resist. My advice is to steer away from gimmick-type machines of this sort and stick with the standard 5-coin single-line machines.

5. BEGIN WITH RELATIVELY SMALL BETS

Regardless of what machine price you choose, determine your range of play and start at the bottom. Most players have a range of 25 cents, 50 cents, and one dollar. If your range is a little lower than that, start with a 5-cent machine if you're playing in a casino that offers them. If you can afford to start higher, you should because nickel machines have the highest hold percentage of all denominations. Still, if that's all you can do, that's where you start.

6. MOVE UP TO HIGHER MACHINE PRICES AS YOU CONTINUE TO WIN

You can utilize the advantages of a progression this way. If you've won a considerable amount on a quarter machine, move up to a 50-cent machine. If a dollar machine has paid off very well for you, why not try a $5 machine in the high-roller pit? But use common sense: If the move up immediately sours, what are you going to do? You either drop back to the bottom price of your range or you quit. It's not complicated. Quitting isn't complicated.

7. PLAY IN SESSIONS WITH A SPECIFIC LOSS LIMIT PER SESSION

When you reach your loss limit, the session is over. Take a break. Take a long break! Setting loss limits makes all the sense in the world. Setting win limits makes no sense at all. If you're winning, keep playing. Play for as long as you win. Winning streaks come along so rarely that you must really take advantage when it happens. Remember, always set a limit on your losses, but let your winnings run!

8. STAY AWAY FROM DOUBLE-UP MACHINES

Some machines today allow you to parlay your winning wager with a "double-up" feature that gives you the option of doubling a win (a double-or-nothing bet). If you lose it, you lose your winnings and your bet. In most cases, the house picks up an extra 8 percent on this wager. No strategy will work against a rip-off like that!

9. PLAY ONLY THOSE MACHINES CLEARLY MARKED "ALL HANDS DEALT FROM 52-CARD DECK"

Although there has been sporadic concern expressed by seasoned players that some machine percentages may be skewed by additional microprocessor control, I doubt the validity of those concerns, but I must admit that I only play machines that display the disclaimer noted. If you have been dealt three kings, you want to know that you have two shots (two cards would be discarded) at beating one in 47 odds of finding that last king. You don't want to know that there might be "additional" programming that cuts the odds of making your four-of-a-kind.

10. AVOID SPEEDING

Here's another item we covered earlier. I'm sure you now know how damaging a fast game speed can be. So slow down and enjoy yourself. I've always believed that most players really don't want to play fast but they feel pressured to win or pressured to "get even." Everyone has internal regulators. If your biological clock simply runs too fast, let it wind down before you play; otherwise, you might find that gambling poses a destructive conflict for you. And don't forget that a relaxed pace helps reduce long-term exposure. In any negative-expectation game, the faster (or longer) you play, the more likely you will lose.

11. NEVER PLAY WHEN YOU'RE TIRED OR UPSET

This is particularly true if you're playing a skill game such as video poker, but no matter which game you play, being tired or upset can lead to serious errors of discipline. Attitudes change when you're not sharp and alert. Why risk a serious financial setback? It will just give you something else to be upset about.

12. IF YOU CAN'T AFFORD TO LOSE IT, DON'T BET IT

Yes, you've heard this expression before. Although it's become a worn out cliché, I would like to restore it to its full faith and vigor. Abide by it every time you put your bankroll together, every time you reach into your wallet, and every time you make a wager!

A SHORT NOTE FOR REEL SLOT PLAYERS

Although this chapter is devoted to video poker, the skill game among slots, I want to close with a special winning secret for reel-type slot players, too. Players marvel at these gaudy games, the simplicity of them all, not caring much about the percentages—and rightly so, for how could they know? How could they know indeed! Read on.

Many years ago, casinos were saddled with a myth among slot players that probably cost them millions of dollars. It was widely believed in those days that machines placed near the entrances to a casino and at the ends of aisles, or anywhere that people congregated, were the better-paying machines. The myth grew to unmanageable proportions for casino operators, when claims became even more exaggerated that certain types of machines in these locations paid out more than they held. It was said that you could identify these "special" machines by listening to the sound they made when paying out jackpots. The louder the noise, the better the payback. Well, it was all a myth, of course, but here's what happened next.

Players who milked these "blessed" machines and came away empty assumed that all the other machines in the casino were worse. After all, if the good machines weren't paying, what would you expect from the rest? Soon, the casinos got drift of the problem. It was too big to counter, so they gave in. Better paying machines were actually installed in key locations to satisfy the myth and keep the players playing *all* the machines. These "up front" machines essentially became loss leaders, to use a retail term.

Today, there are several casinos, particularly those run by the same large corporation, that continue the practice. So, a myth that was truly a myth became reality.

Oh, the power of slot players!

6 ATTACKING TEXAS HOLD'EM

With so many poker books on the market these days, it's easy to get caught up in a tangle of advice that may confuse you. Many of these books are written by the very pros you wish to emulate. But what I find interesting about most of them is the distinct lack of key advice—the secrets, if you will—that the pros apparently don't want you to know about. Or perhaps the best at the game are just a bit too presumptuous of your skills. What you'll often read are tips that fall under the categories of "Common Sense" and "I Already Know That" while other books are too complicated for even seasoned players.

We all know the pros can play. The question is: Can they teach? Can they make winners out of beginners? I've been teaching players how to win at all gambling endeavors, including poker, for nearly thirty years. I know how to play. I know how to win. But most of all, I know how to teach, so expect solid advice that can make you a winner even if you're a beginner.

Probably the worst advice I've ever read in a poker book came from a top pro: "You can't win if you don't play." Boy, is that bad advice or what? It sends a mixed message that is misinterpreted more often than not. "Hmm, maybe I should play this marginal hand," the new player thinks. Maybe, but probably not. Amateurs tend to call too many bets; they don't fold as often as they should. Here's my advice about advice: Successful playing and successful teaching are clearly two different things.

Before we get into the secrets of winning at the poker table, let's review the basics of the game so that you know exactly how to play.

HOW TO PLAY THE GAME

Texas hold'em is played either as a **limit** game or a **no-limit** game. Most poker rooms in casinos around the country spread both types of hold'em games. In **cash** games or **live** games, you can buy more chips when you need to, compared with **tournaments**, where players must leave the game when they run out of chips. Most hold'em tournaments these days are no-limit hold'em, while both no-limit and limit hold'em cash games are typically spread.

There's a huge difference between cash games and tournaments.

NO-LIMIT HOLD'EM TOURNAMENTS

In no-limit hold'em tournaments (as well as cash games), you can bet up to the amount of chips you have in front of you. You can bet all of your chips if you like. It's where the commonly heard phrase **all-in** comes from. In no-limit hold'em tournaments, all players start with the same number of chips for their **buy-in** (the amount it costs to enter the tournament) and are given special tournament chips to play with. Winners are determined by their order of finish. You can't cash in your chips for real money as you would do in a cash game.

Your ranking as the tournament goes along is determined by what is called your **chip count**. If you have 2,000 in chips at the end of two hours, for example, and 23 players have more chips than you have, you're sitting in 24th place and most likely need to improve your position in order to win money. As a general rule, the more players in the tournament, the more places are paid. Many small tournaments pay only the top nine places, while large events can have more than 500 cash winners. As long as you have chips in front of you, you're still in the tournament. The **blinds** (forced bets) continually increase in tournaments, so you can't just sit back and play only the best hands. That's the rub—and that's what makes tournament action so exciting. It's also why so many top pros are often seen at the final table in major televised tournaments. They know how to play weak hands; they have to know because they eventually have to play them. Everyone does. The growing blinds and the diminishing number of players at the table lend an ever-changing complexion to the game's strategy.

LIMIT HOLD'EM CASH GAMES

Unlike tournaments, cash games have set blinds that do not change from the minute you sit down till the minute you walk away. The amount of the blinds is tied in with the betting structure of a particular game. Let's say you're playing a $3/$6 limit hold'em game. Although the dollar amounts suggest a range of betting from a low to a high limit, these dollar values actually represent the amounts you must wager for the four rounds of betting.

For the first two rounds, your bets must be at least $3. For the final two rounds, your bets must be at least $6. You can't bet less, but you can bet more by **raising** (increasing) the bet. However, the raise must be the same structured amount. If a player before you bet $3 and you want to stay in the game, you have to **call** (match) that player's bet by also betting $3. Depending on the strength of your hand, you might want to raise $3 (for a total of $6), which means that the bet increases to $6 for the next player, who must match the bet if he wants to stay in the game. The player who initially bet $3 will have to toss in another $3 (when it's his turn again) to continue playing. If you don't at least call a bet, you must **fold** (surrender) your hand, which means you're out of action until the next hand is dealt.

The casino provides a dealer who shuffles and deals the cards, verifies the bets, settles disputes, and calls the winning hands. The casino dealer also rotates a **button** (a flat round disc) around the table in a clockwise direction every time a new hand is dealt. The player with the button is the last to play, meaning he can weigh all the actions of the other players before acting on his or her own hand.

POSTING THE BLINDS

Your **position** at the table is determined by where you sit in relation to the button. The two players sitting directly to the left of the player on the button are in tough positions, since it's their responsibility to get the engine running by posting the **blinds** (mandatory bets) for the first round of betting on each deal. Before the dealer begins, the first player to the left makes a forced bet called the **small blind**. The player to the left of the small blind has to make the other forced bet called the **big blind**. The terms button, small blind, and big blind can also refer to the players sitting in those positions.

Usually, the amount of the big blind is equal to the smaller of the two limits that define the game. In our $3/$6 game, for example, the big blind is $3. The small blind is generally half that amount when the value can be halved in even dollars, but since a $3/$6 game is played with dollar chips, the small blind is cut to $1. In a $4/$8 game, the blinds are easy to figure: The big blind is $4 and the small blind is $2.

When you first sit down, you probably won't be in one of the blind positions, so the dealer will ask you if you want to **post**; that is, put an amount equal to the big blind in front of you. If you don't post, most casinos don't allow you to play until the blind positions reach you. Their reasoning is that you might be getting some "free" hands to play without having to go through the forced-bet positions.

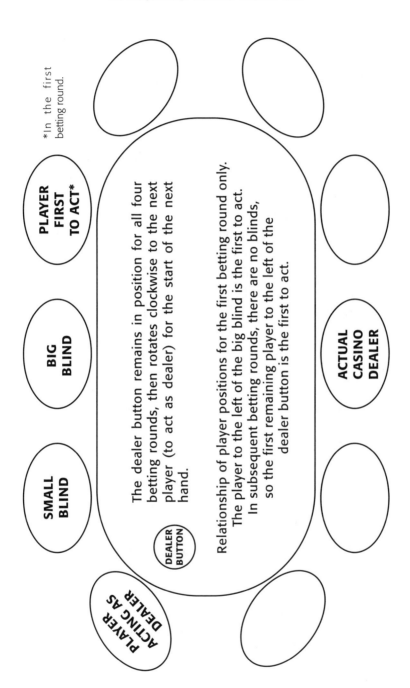

*In the first betting round.

PLAYER FIRST TO ACT*

BIG BLIND

SMALL BLIND

DEALER BUTTON

PLAYER ACTING AS DEALER

ACTUAL CASINO DEALER

The dealer button remains in position for all four betting rounds, then rotates clockwise to the next player (to act as dealer) for the start of the next hand.

Relationship of player positions for the first betting round only. The player to the left of the big blind is the first to act. In subsequent betting rounds, there are no blinds, so the first remaining player to the left of the dealer button is the first to act.

THE FOUR BETTING ROUNDS

THE FIRST BETTING ROUND: PREFLOP

With both blinds posted, the dealer delivers one card face down to each player around the table, and then delivers a second facedown card to each player. These two cards are your **hole** cards, also called **pocket** cards. They comprise your **hand**, and are for your eyes only. Be careful not to expose your hand to players sitting beside you. Most players like to pull their cards close to the edge of the table (but not off the table) and then slide them apart just enough to be able to see both card values as they bend the top edges of the cards upward with their thumbs while cupping the cards with their hands.

The player to the left of the big blind is first to act, and must decide whether to call the big blind (match the $3 bet), raise to $6, or fold his cards by sliding them face down toward the dealer. The next player goes through these same options, and so on until the betting gets around to the small blind. If the small blind wants to stay in the game, he needs to match the size of the big blind. In our $3/$6 game, that means he must put in another $2.

Don't toss your bets onto the table in some reckless fashion, but place them directly in front of you. After all players have acted, the dealer gathers all the bets and places them near the center of the table to create the **pot** (the total bets) that you will be competing for.

THE SECOND BETTING ROUND: THE FLOP

The dealer begins the second betting round by dealing three cards face up in the center of the table. These cards are called the **flop** and are the first three of five community cards that all players can use—along with their hole cards—to make their best possible poker hand.

Betting begins with the first active player to the left of the dealer button. Some players likely folded on the preflop round, so there are probably fewer players to compete against. The first player to bet in this second round has an additional betting option that wasn't available in the first round: He can **check**, which means to pass on making a bet. A player could not check in the first round because of the blind bets already in the pot. That is, you can't check after someone has already bet; you can only check if no one has bet before you.

Because so many players in low-limit games usually stay in the game to see the flop, regardless of the strength of their pocket cards, the flop generally sees the most folds. "It only costs me a few bucks to see the flop," is the logic that many players use when they call the big blind before the flop, but it's a dangerous notion. Those "few bucks" will eat them up in short order with that kind of ill-advised reasoning—but they came to play, and play they do.

THE THIRD BETTING ROUND: THE TURN

The pivotal third round begins with the dealer placing a fourth community card on the table, called the **turn** card. The significant feature of this round is the increase in the betting limit. In our theoretical $3/$6 game, all bets are now $6, not $3 as they were in the first two rounds. If the first active player left of the button tosses in $6 and the next player raises $6, if you're the next player to act, you have to call $12 if you want to stay in the game.

Serious money? If a $3/$6 game is your speed, yes, $12 is serious. But hear me out on this. Money values are relative, I know, but why wait until the third round to take it seriously? Sadly, it's the way many rookie players play the game. If that $6 raise spooked you, you might want to search out a $2/$4 game. Better yet, I suggest you rack up experience and learn from it.

Develop street smarts and basic book knowledge to gain the confidence to play at higher limits, not lower.

THE FOURTH BETTING ROUND: THE RIVER

The fourth and final round of betting starts with the dealer placing a fifth card face up directly beside the turn card. This card, called the **river** card, will pretty much tell you whether it's time to go for the jugular or limp out of the game. And that's a rather accurate appraisal of your choices because, at this stage of the game, you're virtually assured of significant betting action. You've gauged the possible hands of your opponents and hopefully, you've got a good idea about their strengths and weaknesses. More often than not, it's a fight to the finish with only those players holding strong hands. There is little **bluffing** (representing a better hand than you actually have) in a low-limit game, so be prepared for battle.

After the betting is completed, if more than one player remains, there is a **showdown** to determine who has the best hand and therefore wins the pot. However, if one player has bounced all the others out of the game before then, he wins the pot without even having to show his cards.

TYPICAL $3-$6 LIMIT HOLD'EM FORMAT			
BETTING ROUND	CARDS DEALT	BET/RAISE AMOUNT	BLINDS
1	2 (Pocket)	$3	$1/$3
2	3 (Flop)	$3	—
3	1 (Turn)	$6	—
4	1 (River)	$6	—

STRATEGY CONCEPTS

HOW GOOD IS YOUR HAND?

Whether you're playing a limit or no-limit game, knowing the relative value of your hand is the key strategy of Texas hold'em. The worth of your hand is always relative to the conditions at a particular table at a particular time. Never think of hole-card values as absolutes. I've listed starting hand values in the following chart, which includes the best hands from A-A down to J-10 in relative order of their strength. If you're a beginner, this list should make you feel more confident in deciding which hands to play, especially when you're playing at a full table.

But remember that these values are not cut in stone. The number of players, the overall strength of these players and particularly their real-time actions, and your chip standing (in a tournament) all affect your decisions to play or fold even the relatively strong hands that I've listed. This is why the game is called poker and not blackjack, where absolutes abound. They do not abound at the poker table—no, poker is a thinking game. And most times, what pro players are thinking about is whether or not they want to buck the absolutes or perhaps cuddle up to a relatively weak hand. It's what makes the game so unpredictable. To the extent that you can break through a player's facade of unpredictability, you have acquired an edge.

THE BEST STARTING HANDS		
GROUP 1	**GROUP 2**	**GROUP 3**
A-A	J-J	K-J
K-K	K-Q	K-10
A-K	A-J	Q-J
Q-Q	10-10	Q-10
A-Q	A-10	J-10

If the unpaired cards are suited, that's an obvious plus. Surprisingly, however, the ranking of the higher-value hands does not change significantly whether the cards are suited or offsuit. Many players in low-limit games routinely stay in to see the flop with almost any two cards, a tendency that tends to skew our starting hand values. And the fact that so many players usually call to see the flop in lower limit games accounts for the fewer number of heads-up contests in cash games compared to tournaments. As you can now appreciate, hand values are essentially empirical and often debated. There are simply too many variables to assign an absolute ranking.

There is a general progression among these top 15 hands, although it is a mild one indeed. In theory, the first group of starting hands is your best ammo against any number of players, of any skill level. Fire away! The second group would seem to be the same; however, holding 10-10 against a full table of top players might make you stop and think (and it should). Against only four or five players, top guns or not, it's a different story: Play 'em! The third group of strong hands usually gives you the green light against three or four players. But you might also want to fire them off against a full table too, depending on the composition of your opponents.

3 FACTORS THAT IMPACT THE STRENGTH OF YOUR HAND

Top players understand these three factors and apply them in terms of odds rather than absolutes. The three main variables that impact the strength of your hand are the likelihood of getting beat with an overcard; the high value of your cards; and the number of players in the game. Let's discuss these factors one at a time.

1. OVERCARD VULNERABILITY

Let's say you're holding 6-6, certainly not a strong hand, even though pairs are always tempting to play. It's likely that several players at a full or nearly full table will have at least one card in the hole that's higher than a 6. That card could easily pair up with the **overcard** (a card that is higher than the highest card in your hand) on the **board** (the community cards) and beat you. You have to survive five shots (the five cards on the board) at beating your lowly 6's. The only community card that could improve your hand is another 6. However, in a heads-up tournament game where you have only one remaining opponent, it's a different story. Your low pair might be top hand! After all, you only have one other hand to beat, not eight or nine.

Of course, there's always the likelihood that another player at a full table holds a higher pair. If the community cards don't help you—and it's unlikely they will—you're beaten right out of the gate. The only real hope with such a marginal hand is that other players do not pair up, or if they do, they pair below your 6's. That's a lot to hope for.

2. HIGH-VALUE CARD STRENGTH

Obviously, an ace is the best card to have in the pocket. If the other card is also high—let's say it's a king—that's even better. If the other card is another ace, you've got the best possible hole cards.

But if you stay in with a 6-5 **offsuit** (different suits), these certainly are not high cards and can easily be beaten. Your only hope is to make two pair or get lucky and fill a straight. If the 6-5 is **suited** (the same suit), that may change the complexion of your hand since a flush also becomes a possibility. However, making flush draws or attempting to fill straights should not be first on your list. You are first interested in numerical values, a more likely contributor to a win.

3. NUMBER AND QUALITY OF PLAYERS

As the number of active players decreases, you have fewer chances of getting beaten by a lucky draw. You can often make the assumption at a full table that some other player has a stronger hand than you do, but you certainly cannot make that assumption at a **short** table; that is, a table with six or few players. The fewer the players, the fewer the shots that can be taken at you.

Whenever a game is played short, the value of pocket cards changes. At a full table, I'll toss 10-9 suited, but I might play it in a short-handed limit hold'em game. And in a no-limit hold'em tournament, my 10-9 is a definite go if the blinds are building and players are thinning out. You don't necessarily need the big guns to beat half an army!

A further consideration in evaluating your hole cards is the type of game you're playing. Limit hold'em cash games and no-limit hold'em tournament have inherent idiosyncrasies that dictate playing them in distinctly different ways. Let's look at each one separately.

TIPS FOR PLAYING LIMIT HOLD'EM CASH GAMES

The type of game you're playing makes a difference. Are you playing in a low-stakes game or a high-stakes game? Players in low-stakes games tend to play out their hands, so there is rarely any real playing strategy to contend with. The best hand wins—often it's that simple. But higher limit games such as $10/$20 hold'em are usually won or lost by using sound betting strategies, even with somewhat weaker hands. Part of the strategy is letting other players make mistakes. Make them fold when they should stay, and stay when they should fold. To do this, you must take control of the game. Most players don't raise as often as they should; so instead of calling, try raising to take control of the betting.

The quality of players is of significant importance to hand valuation in a limit game. Are you up against good players or beginners? My choice has always been to play a progression of limit games, starting with $4/$8 and moving up through $10/$20 and perhaps to $20/$40 if my success continues. The varying quality of players I run into along the way is quite remarkable—usually, the higher the stakes the better the players. A key to winning is how quickly I can discern the abilities of my opponents.

In either a limit or no-limit game, players tend to overvalue suited pocket cards unless they are high cards. Most hands are won with high pairs, two pair, or **trips** (three-of-a-kind). With fewer players, many hands are won on just high card. Always make this a key consideration in evaluating your hole cards.

Beware of playing too many hands and calling too many bets. Folding is tough for many beginners to do. Why? Because they came to *play*! They don't want to just sit there watching other players play. But poker isn't a boxing match—poker is a game of strategy. Sure, there's always the hope of catching the right card on the river, but poker isn't won on hope, it's won on skill and discipline: the discipline to play only three or four hands out of ten. Actually, there's plenty to do while you're out of a hand, and I don't mean playing with your chips. Work on studying the other players. You'll get a different sense of their playing habits when you're only observing instead of participating. So what does all of this say about average players? It says that they go to the poker rooms of casinos across the country to play. Apparently, winning is secondary.

TIPS FOR PLAYING NO-LIMIT HOLD'EM TOURNAMENTS

In tournaments, the blinds increase at predetermined intervals that range from 20 or 30 minutes in small tournaments to two hours in events like the World Series of Poker. The escalating price of the blinds can have a huge impact on the hands you play in no-limit hold'em tournaments. Until the blinds become significant, however, play in the same manner as you would play a higher-priced cash game. For many players, this means taking a conservative approach, both in the hands they play and the way they play them. Such players are keyed to two things: staying in the game and building up rations.

There is great value in patience—sometimes you just need to bide your time. As important as patience is, however, don't confuse it with being timid. When the time comes, you need to hustle, you need to find your aggression knob and turn it up. You can't let the fear of losing keep you out of a decent hand, yet I see it happen all the time. If you're the timid type, tournament no-limit hold'em is not your game. Knowing when to attack and when to lay back is what separates the pros from the wannabes—and not just in poker either. This rare trait is a hallmark of success in any competition. As Abraham Lincoln said, "Things may come to those who wait, but only the things left by those who hustle."

As the blinds increase, you'll reach the point where you will have to play weak hands to remain in the game. It is usually always late in the game when the best players make their moves. You may find yourself in a heated head-to-head battle, playing nearly every hand just to prevent the other player from **stealing** the blinds (winning the blinds because the other player folds). Remember what I said earlier: The reason you see many of the same pros at numerous final tables is because they know how to play weak hands. Skillful bluffs are one obvious edge, but understanding the habits of the other players is just as important. And don't think luck doesn't count—take all you can get!

Some nonprofessionals who make it into the later rounds of a tournament will switch gears to an ultraconservative strategy. With a dwindling stack of chips, they've mentally accepted a 15th place finish, for example, and a small piece of the prize pool. Not the attitude of a winner! Sometimes you have to play tough hands. A good poker player can rank these hands; tough hands are certainly not all the same. For example, 3-2 suited is weaker than 7-6 suited on two counts. Obviously, the card values are smaller, but there also is a better chance of making a straight with a 7-6, even though making a straight should be a secondary consideration. The weaker 3-2 will only team up with a 4-5-6 or an A-4-5, whereas the 7-6 can team up with 3-4-5, 4-5-8, 5-8-9, and 8-9-10.

Of course, many tough hands don't even give you the possibility of a straight draw. A hand such as 10-4 won't make it the easy way (using both pocket cards) because there's too big a gap between the card values. The thin straight possibilities you have only allow you to use one of your pocket cards. You would need to get lucky with, say, A-K-Q-J on the board. Fat chance! With a hand like 10-4 off-suit, you can only hope to pair up, preferably with another 10, but a better "hope" is that the other players left in the game have hands just as shaky as yours! There's no question that being forced to play tough hands in the late stage of a tournament is a gamble you have to take in no-limit hold'em.

The biggest fault of most beginner tournament players is a failure to fold. In the later rounds, these amateurs have a different excuse for not folding: They've stuck around for most of the game, made an investment they hate to walk away from, and actually feel obligated to stay in the fight. If you're still chewing on my mention of playing three or four hands out of ten, folding 60 to 70 percent of the time, let me give you some hard facts: The statistics on folding in major tournaments versus small tournaments is rather telling. Nearly 70 percent of the hands in the early rounds of big tournaments (against full tables) are folded, yet only 50 percent of early-round hands are tossed in smaller tournaments. I don't know the statistic for low-stakes limit games, but I'm willing to bet that it's no more than 40 percent. According to those who keep watch over the actions of professional players, folding about 65 to 70 percent of hands is about the right ratio.

LEARNING TO READ YOUR OPPONENTS' TELLS

Before you play, take every opportunity to size up the other players. In poker parlance, that means getting a read on your opponents' **tells**, any quirks in their betting habits that they inadvertently show. Most players have a tendency to not change their style, so what you might learn from observing their habits can work for you over a potentially long session at the table.

Earlier I mentioned that the dealer asks new players in a limit cash game if they want to post. Players who answer yes can play immediately. Players who answer no must wait until the blinds reach their position at the table. And that's just fine—it gives you a little time to unwind, but more important, you'll get some time to watch the other players play poker. You'd be surprised how much you can pick up in just a short time.

In the days when I played frequently in downtown Las Vegas casinos (my favorite stomping grounds), I remember a player who would always buy in, sit down (there was rarely a wait in those days), and then just study the players before he even stacked his chips. He might sit out half a dozen hands before he played, but he was making his presence felt. Can you relate to this tactic? Everyone got to know him since he was a "regular," but there was always a fresh face or two to study. And this player, who became a star player on tour decades later, would tend to rile these new players with the way he stared them down.

I'll never forget the following quote from this great player: "People think that poker is a game of luck and skill. Well, more than that, it's a game of remembering. I never forget faces, I never forget names, and I can tell you everything you need to know to beat those players because I know every little tell (playing habit) they have. I store it all away."

The concept of getting reads on other players is fundamental to poker. Of course, it's is a two-pronged attack. You must learn how to develop your own mystique too, as well as jam the airwaves when other players try to tune you in. The idea is to get a read on them, but not let them get a read on you. Players who won't let other players penetrate their shields are ahead of the game. You want to be a mystery to other players; you want to frustrate them. Try to become an unpredictable, hard-to-read combatant by mixing up your actions well enough that no one has an inkling whether you have rockets (aces) in the pocket or 10's that need a booster.

"When I stare down other players," my poker buddy also said, "I'm careful to make it a one-way street. I want to get inside their heads, but I don't want them to get inside mine!" Few poker players without this psychological edge are successful. It's that simple. So how do you see through the other players' masks and how do you hide behind yours? A key question that deserves a key answer.

What has made televised poker tournaments so successful is showing the audience the players' hole cards. Without this technology, poker tournaments probably would have been relegated to the ratings of hotdog eating contests. Knowing all the hole cards makes tournaments all the more exciting, and it also may make some TV viewers think they're more of an expert than they are. But what they may not know is that some players might as well have a TV monitor right on the table in front of them! What some players can discern through sheer observation is remarkable. Subtle movements can indicate the strength or weakness of players' hands. Most rookie players overly exhibit these tells in the act of bluffing, which is why few can successfully pull it off.

Many of the pros learned about their own tells by having other pros watch them. It's hard for most players to detect their own tells. Some will even go to the extreme of video taping a mock session. It's common practice for pros that play on TV to tape the programs to not only look for other players' tells, but to detect their own as well. If you haven't yet had the opportunity to tape yourself on a televised tournament, then go ahead and tape a mock session with your friends. Study the tape over and over. You'll be surprised how many easy tells are there for the picking. Do your eyes light up when you see the card you need? Does your chin drop when you miss your draw? Whether you study a tape or a player at a live game, this experience can only build in your favor.

Many top players believe that detecting tells is an innate quality, not a learned skill, but I find that comment highly suspect. It's arguable, but I believe that the skill can be developed. For that reason, I've always recommended that poker buddies get together and instead of just playing around for a few bucks, actually spend some time working on tell detection. That's right: Work with your friends to hone your skills. The pros do it, so why don't you try it? The players who are really into physical analysis tend to perform better, regardless. That's a fact. One player that I used to play with claimed that he had worked on it for so long that he had developed a new sense (would that be the sixth?) that not only helped him in poker but in his business world too. He called it "super vision," and he called upon it often: Is that guy telling the truth? Does he really have a better offer? Is that the best price I can get?

DEALING WITH ADVERSITY

If you play golf, you know how it feels to shoot a horrible round. A bad day is, well, a bad day! Similarly, despite all the psychological edges you can muster and all the knowledge you may have accumulated, it's still darned tough to win at poker if you don't get the cards. You need good cards—let's not dance around it! What you want to see in the pocket are aces and face cards—lots of paint. And if you're not getting those good cards, there's no book in the world that can help you. I don't care how good you are, if it's just not your day, you're going to get beaten. We all have bad days at poker—but the key is how we deal with them.

Knowing how to deal with adversity is the mark of a successful player. Many players, experienced or not, don't have a clue. The typical response is to keep pulling the trigger when they're out of bullets. Click, click, click. "You can't force the cards," to repeat an old gambling axiom. Sure, you can try to outfox the other players with weak hands but that won't get you through the day. But there is a surefire way to end a losing session. When you're out of ammo, the smartest thing to do is to holster your weapon and retreat. There will always be another poker game to play, so just retreat and plan for the next battle. If you're stuck in a tournament, you can only hope for a better result the next time you enter. If you're in a cash game, the answer is easy: Rise from your chair, go home, and wait for a better game tomorrow.

Wouldn't it be nice if you knew what you were getting into before you plunked down your money? A smattering of top players I know seem to have a strangely instinctive, intuitive sense about their day over that first cup of coffee. Call it premonition, call it timing, call it whatever you want to, but I give tons of credit to those rare players who have such a keen sense of awareness. Simply put, they know when to play—and they know when not to play.

Here's another thing they do: They know how to play the game with total concentration. In a remarkable change from the early days of poker when the game was treated as if it were a golf match, poker tournaments today are filled with excitement and noise. Top poker players have a knack for tuning out the din of a noisy poker room. It's not chess, but there's a considerable amount of strategy required. Don't look around the room. Who cares what's out there? The action is right in front of you! Keep any interference at bay. And while you're at it, learn how to psych yourself up for a big game, even if it isn't that big. You'll play better! There's plenty to think about, much to remember, and certainly some tough decisions to make.

Here's a quote I'll always remember from a poker pro who said it best: "All I think about is poker. Even before the game, I'm playing back old hands, recalling the players, the right moves, the wrong moves to get me in the right gear. At the table, you could light a firecracker behind me and I wouldn't hear it. Poker—that's all I'm thinking about when the chips are down."

12 TIPS FROM THE POKER PROS

Poker room managers know the games inside and out. Their wisdom in understanding the right moves at the hold'em tables and their willingness to help new players are highlighted in the following tips I gleaned years ago from many of the top poker room managers across the country. Heed their advice.

TIP #1

"New players don't protect their hands. They either forget to or they don't know how. Put your hand on the table directly in front of you and protect it with a chip marker (one of your chips) placed on top of your cards. Otherwise, if another player throws his cards away and they land on your cards, you have a dead hand."

Vito, poker room supervisor, Ameristar Casino, Kansas City

TIP #2

"Betting out of turn is a problem I see. By jumping ahead, a player could force someone to fold. And some players do it on purpose to intimidate a player to drop out of the game. Something else beginners should know: A card dropped on the floor is dead. Drop 'em both, you lose 'em both. Technically, you're not out of the game."

Ray, pit manager, Bally's, Atlantic City

TIP #3

"If a player needs to leave the table to eat, we give them up to 30 minutes, but our rules are a little different for any other reason. If the button goes around the table three times, we page. If the player doesn't answer, the seat is given up. When a player takes a break, the player's chips must stay on the table. If the chips are picked up, the player has lost his seat. We're "table stakes" here. So taking stakes off the table ends the play. We're also very personalized with players, having only five tables. I always suggest that beginners find a smaller room like ours where they can be helped their first time out."

Dick, poker room supervisor, Atlantis Casino, Reno

TIP #4

"Poker is like an investment. Always protect your investment—your cards and your money—by managing it wisely. Only play the best value hands, either in live games (limit hold'em) or no-limit tournaments, where the blinds can sometimes force you to play weaker hands. But depending on how much you have in front of you in a no-limit game, you can still bet value hands much of the time. And know the players you're going up against, especially if your best value-hand is weaker than you would like."

Eric, poker room manager, Arizona Charlie's, Las Vegas

TIP #5

"I see it all the time: Beginners, even veterans, complain that they're running bad and they blame it on bad luck. So I pose this question to them: Are you sure you're good enough? Maybe you need to improve your game: the statistics, emotions, the psychological part of the game. If you continually lose, don't try to convince yourself you're just unlucky. That's a dangerous copout. You're kidding yourself. You need a certain temperament, a certain discipline for gambling. And you need patience. Do you have these qualities?"

Kamell, poker room shift manager, Bellagio, Las Vegas

TIP #6

"Most beginners show a tendency to want to play too many hands. My advice: Be conservative. At a low-limit game, good starting hands are paramount because it's hard to bluff. In the long run, better players win because they play better starting hands. The worst starting hand is hard to say—depends on the game, who's in the game, whether you're winning or losing. Tell your readers to keep records of the results of their play of certain hands, and win/loss records too. You can really learn from your notes."

Jack, poker lead floor, Bicycle Casino, Bell Gardens, CA

TIP #7

"Patience is most important. New players think two bucks isn't much; next thing you know, you're 'two-bucked' to death. It's frustrating in low-limit games that everyone plays out their cards, so you better wait for a good hand. We get better players at $4/$8, but you know what? You still need good hands. I tell beginners that just because you have two suited cards, two hearts for example, it doesn't necessarily mean it's a good hand. We have six tables going and they're all Texas hold'em. A couple of stud games might go, but everyone wants to play hold'em!"

Deanna, poker room manager, Cactus Pete's, Jackpot, NV

TIP #8

"To play in a small tournament is better than a limit game for beginners because you get to start with more chips. For a $35 buy-in, players get $1,500 in chips and valuable experience that could last for several sessions. Playing with your own money at a limit game could end up costing a player many times that amount. Our $35 buy-in tournaments have five tables, that's 55 players (11 players at a table), and we pay the top four places. Bigger tournaments, like our $100 buy-in event, pay 15 places."

Brenda, pit manager, Chinook Winds Casino, Lincoln City, OR

TIP #9

"There's nothing more fun than pushing out all of your chips and doubling up in a no-limit hold'em tournament. We do a lot of $25-buy-in, no-limit tournaments that give you 1,000 chips. A $10 "rebuy" gets you another thousand. Tournaments last about five hours and are much different from a structured limit game. My advice: During the first three or four rounds, hang low. Tournaments are a process of elimination, so let the field bust each other out. Then the cream comes to the top and you have to start playing some good poker. Don't get caught up in burning off your chips early."

James, poker room manager, Colorado Belle Casino, Laughlin, NV

TIP #10

"First, get a Texas hold'em computer game; play on that for a while because it's the easiest way to learn without losing money. Then, once you feel comfortable with the game, go to a casino and play in a live game, a low-limit game like $2/$4. Or try a no-limit hold'em game with $1/$2 blinds, because that's what everyone's looking for. There are no betting limits, but you only have to start with a $2 call of the big blind. It's the same action as a big tournament, but no big risk. The game is table stakes with a minimum buy-in of $50, but most players go in for $100 to $200. Low-limit tournaments with no-limit action are good for beginners, too. Internet gambling is okay, but first get some experience on the computer game."

Brad, acting day-shift supervisor, Gold Strike Casino, Tunica,
MS

TIP #11

"Players come in expecting a no-limit game since that's all they see on TV, but we have a lot of structured limit hold'em games, and occasionally a no-limit game, or a pot-limit game (where you can bet up to what's in the pot). We get some players who try 7-card stud games, but mostly the beginners want Texas hold'em because it's faster, has a lot of action, and it's what they see on TV. But some beginners who sit down at a stud game like it. My advice, though, is to play what you're looking for; don't try a different game you might not know just because a seat's open."

Alberto, poker room supervisor, Harrah's East Chicago Casino,
IN

TIP #12

"Believe it or not, we see players come in who don't even know the ranking of the hands. They don't know what hands to play or fold. They're coming here prematurely; every day we have to help teach these beginners how to play, and we don't mind doing that at all. TV tournaments sometimes give new players the wrong impression; the misbehavior of some pros, for example, is the worst thing. Players need to know game etiquette. They can't run around the tables and act like kids. They want to be like the pros, but sometimes we have to calm them down."

Doc, Poker room supervisor, The Nugget, Sparks, NV

SUMMARY OF GOOD ADVICE

Many of the poker room managers I talked to couldn't believe the number of new players who walk in with a completely distorted view of the rules of the game. They've been playing in private games with their friends, making up a lot of their own rules, and then they step into a structured casino game and feel totally lost.

Speaking for many of the poker experts, the advice is clear: Learn the game the right way from the outset. And even though all the managers I spoke with indicated that they are more than happy to help beginners, it is clearly incumbent on all new players to learn the game first, maybe by practicing on a computer game as one manager suggested, or forging an intimate relationship with a good poker book. Experience playing in a live game is an absolute must—but first get the knowledge you need to make the most of that experience.

7 A WINNER'S NOTEBOOK

Let me tell you what I do, and what I don't do, as part of the general plan I follow when I gamble, regardless of the game. I've covered some of these important points earlier, but allow me to review them for you in a more organized fashion. Besides, picking up on my advice a second time can only help you in your pursuit of victory.

WHAT I DO: 6 ESSENTIALS

1. **I always watch a game before I play.**
   My "stakeout" might end up with a walk—in fact, most often it does—if the game doesn't suit my style of play. This is the time to let your intuitive senses take charge.

2. **I usually play short sessions.**
   Again, the idea is to strike quickly and run. Obviously, I don't run as long as the dealer is pushing pots to me. I run when an opportunity has ended.

3. **I start each session with the same modest stake, and always begin with wagers at the table-minimum level.**

   My starting stake for each session is $40—never more, never less. It's a discipline that has saved me from ruin more times than you could imagine.

4. **I follow a betting progression designed to ensure that I won't miss out on a fabulous streak of wins.**

   In years past, I missed out on numerous opportunities and vowed that I would never let that happen again. My incremental betting habits have forced me to ride these waves when they roll in. And you know what? Practicing this strategy has taught me more than just taking advantage of rare betting opportunities: It has taught me how to spot them early, and jump on them before other players can sense what's happening.

5. **I exit a session when one of two triggers kicks in: Either I lose two bets in a row, or my stake dwindles to 50 percent of its value.**

   That's right. I not only know how to quit winners, I know how to quit losers. Just as it's important to maximize your winnings, it is equally important to minimize your losses. There are two points worth noting from this important discipline: (1) I will always walk away with at least a significant portion of my original stake; and (2) I will never lose three bets in a row at the same table.

6. **I take frequent breaks.**

   The strict exit rules I follow force me to take breaks. Breaks give me time to cash in chips, making sure I have those two twenties to start my next assault. Breaks from the action can be anything from a stop in the coffee shop to a leisurely walk outdoors. My breaks are not short nor do they bore me. I always enjoy the anticipation of my next session.

WHAT I DON'T DO: 5 NO-NO'S

1. **I'm not a grind player. I don't commandeer a spot at a table and stay there for hours on end. I'm not there to play—I'm there to win!**

   Never get too comfy at the tables. Forget the idea of "settling in." I remember watching a guy peel off ten C-notes and turn them into ten grand in ten minutes. Boy, did he hit 'em quickly! But he didn't leave; he stuck around. Before I left the table, I remember his asking the dealers if he would have any trouble cashing in his high-denomination chips. When I saw him at that same table an hour or so later, he had given back at least half of his win. Later in the day I saw him there again, with nothing but a few piddling chips in front of him.

2. **I never play for comps.**

   Frankly, I don't like the idea of casino bosses even knowing who I am. Comps tend to make players feel a little too cozy with the casino, as if they have established a warm, sporting relationship: "You do this for me, I'll do that for you. Play at this level for this much time, and you'll get this much back in comp rewards." No thank you! I don't want the casino to influence the way I play. Besides, I table hop so often, because of my frequent breaks, that it would be nearly impossible for a casino boss to keep a tab on my play. Understand this: Comps are a casino's most effective trap to lure players into deeper waters than they want to go.

3. **I don't set limits on my winnings, although I do set limits on my losses.**

    It's a point of contention among gaming writers, but I don't see how there can be any dispute. If you're winning, keep playing! And play hard. Winning sessions are not the rule; they are the exception. Learn how to take full advantage.

4. **I don't look down my nose at a token win.**

    Hey, a win is a win! Be happy with it. Even if it's only a few dollars, take it and be thankful. A win beats a loss every time. If you're going to be greedy about it and settle for only large wins, heed one of my favorite gambling maxims: Greed turns winners into losers. Astute gamblers have learned how to take what they can get.

5. **I don't linger.**

    When it's time for me to leave, I leave. And no one knows this better than my wife, Kathy. We leave so expeditiously you'd think the place was on fire! After a full slate of sessions, whether I've won or lost, I know the importance of a quick exit. It's my way of avoiding the temptation to go back for more; or worse, to try to get even. It might sound trite but I consider it one of my top tips: When it's over, it's over! Most gamblers just haven't learned how to pack it up.

15 SMART THINGS WORTH REMEMBERING

1. **I temper my anxiety to gamble.**
   I always schedule something else to do upon my arrival at the casino—a lunch, a meeting, a dip in the pool.
2. **I think positive thoughts.**
   Casinos are full of negative people and negative situations. I avoid them like the plague.
3. **I always have my intuition switch turned on.**
   It could be the most powerful weapon we have. Few people use it.
4. **I leave three things at home: superstitions, systems, and revenge.**
   The first two are obvious. In the third case, revenge, I never think of a casino as owing me anything.
5. **I shop for the best games.**
6. **I never play to impress.**
   Big bets won't make me a better player. Big bets won't change the cards.
7. **I never play on credit.**
   Easy come, easy go.
8. **I know when to be aggressive and when not to.**
   I switch gears often, although I mostly play in my conservative mode.
9. **I take with me precisely the right bankroll for a particular trip, no more and no less.**
10. **I never play the newer casino games.**
    They are designed as rapid-decision affairs with no skill to speak of, and they're fraught with percentages that are too high for me to consider.
11. **I never play if I'm tired or moody or have too many things on my mind.**

12. **I never bet against a trend.**
    Always bet with a streak, never against it.
13. **I make gambling a planned destination trip.**
    I never go gambling on a whim.
14. **I never play on weekends or holidays.**
    I only play on weekdays when I have more choices and more space.
15. **I always focus on my only objective—winning!**

OTHER NOTES FROM THE NOTEBOOK

A. MOST EXCITING BETS

1. Horse Racing
2. Craps
3. Sports

B. SMARTEST BETS

1. At a blackjack table, a double down on 11 with the dealer showing 6, especially if your count shows a great excess of 10-value cards
2. The odds bet on both pass-line and come bets at a craps table, particularly 5 times and 10 times odds
3. A paytable of 9-6 on a jacks-or-better video poker machine

C. DUMBEST BETS

1. Keno
   The more numbers you mark, the dumber the bet!
2. The 5-number bet at the roulette table
   This bet costs you 7.89 percent; all other bets are 5.26 percent. Hardly a bargain!
3. One-roll bets at the craps table
   Especially "Any 7," which has a whopping 16.67 percent house advantage!

D. SMARTEST MOVES

1. Counting cards at blackjack
2. Developing psychological skills at poker
3. Clocking a "single zero" roulette wheel

E. DUMBEST MOVES

1. Never hitting a stiff at a blackjack table
2. Tracking previous numbers at a roulette wheel
3. Playing a nickel slot machine that requires more than 5 coins for a maximum bet

F. SKILL GAMES

1. Poker
2. Horse Racing
3. Sports Betting

The classic skill game is poker, but horse racing and sports betting are certainly skill oriented too. You should know, however, that handicapping horses and sports teams requires a tremendous amount of study and research to be successful over the long term. Video poker and craps also have certain skills associated with them, but these skills are rarely enough to overcome a narrow house edge. The games are more correctly called low-percentage games.

Although this book's title suggests that the games we've covered are vulnerable to the casino, it should be noted that Texas hold'em and other poker games are not really won or lost at the expense of a casino, but at the expense of the players, particularly unskilled players. Casinos routinely take a percentage of the pot in limit games and a percentage of the buy-ins in no-limit tournaments. They really don't care who wins or loses.

Blackjack is a true skill game, however, due to the many recent rule changes and casino countermeasures—and the widespread installation of continuous shufflers—it is less so than before. Because of these factors, instead, I now view blackjack as a strong low-percentage game that can produce an unusual frequency of wins under the right conditions.

For the great majority of players, however, even the bona fide skill games should be considered only as low-percentage games because most players do not play with optimum skill, nor do they exercise discipline to the fullest. But for those few who do, it's money in the bank!

TRAITS OF A PROFESSIONAL PLAYER

When I created this list, the idea going in was to find the raw qualities that seem to define top poker players. But the more I looked at it, the more I realized that the list defines a good gambler in general, not just poker players. How many of these traits do you have?

PROFESSIONAL PLAYER TRAITS		
Passion	Tenacity	Stamina
Courage	Persistence	Experience
Dedication	Focus	Logic
Knowledge	Discipline	Perception

TRAITS OF A ROOKIE PLAYER

Here's a short list of traits that usually work against you in a casino. They help you lose. In fact, these dubious traits may be worth losing altogether.

ROOKIE PLAYER TRAITS		
Ego	Anxiety	Superstition
Greed	Fear	Desperation

A WINNER'S STORY

IF DAVE CAN DO IT...

I started this book with a story about a player who gave up his video poker winnings so that he could have some fun at the dice tables, remember? If you read that story, you learned that losing is the great teacher. But winning can also teach you things, so allow me to end this book with a story about a winner. You'll learn from it too.

Dave Friedman moved to Las Vegas several years ago after quitting his job as a mid-level manager. My old golfing buddy wanted to see if his incredible skill in rating college football teams could turn into a means of making a living. He wanted to gamble legally, so he wisely chose Vegas. I know this guy inside and out. He's a research freak. Put him in a library, spread books all over the table in front of him, and he's in his element. The boon of the Internet has been a blessing for this guy. He navigates the net like Columbus sailed the ocean blue. But newspapers and magazines—sports magazines, of course—are still his bread-and-butter sources.

It's worth noting the way he watches a game: He doesn't watch it like you and I do. He tapes every game he can and studies the plays as if he were one of the coaches of the teams. He has a remarkable sense for figuring out at exactly what level a team will play based on games earlier in the season or, to some extent, the past season. He thinks it's the number one factor in sports handicapping—ranking teams in terms of emotion, desire, and toughness. Not overall, of course, but specifically for the upcoming weekend. A team that crushes a tough opponent one week might be low on his list for the following week. And if you ask him why, he'll give you an hour's worth of reasons.

But let me cut to the chase. Dave has been in Vegas now for about three years. Here's his track record. The first year he was a little nervous and a bit too conservative. He made about $25,000 net after expenses. And, yes, he reported all of it as income. He treated his venture as a business, setting up a plush office in one of his bedrooms at home. Dave's record keeping would knock you over. He hired a bookkeeper to help him stay organized (his only shortfall), to keep the books, and pay the taxes.

The second year was better. He cleared about $75,000. The third year was the charm: Over a quarter-of-a-million dollars!

THE VALUE OF ALERTS

Whether at the poker tables, the racetrack or the sportsbooks, I keep two sets of alerts safely tucked in my wallet that I always refer to. These alerts or signals or whatever you want to call them are always "on," always there to alert me to a situation that can either make me vulnerable or make me a winner. One set is basic to all forms of gambling; the other sets are unique to a particular game. Start thinking about the things that you believe belong on your list.

1. MANAGING MONEY

I suggest you top your basic alert list with the same one that's on top of mine. Keeping your winnings—as obvious as that might sound—should be front and center on every gambler's agenda. When you feel an unwarranted urge to spend a goodly portion of your winnings, you should hear the alert. Is it time to leave the tables, to walk away from the track?

The way I manage my money is two-fold: First, I play off my bankroll in strict limits per game, session, or day, depending on whether I'm betting poker, horses, or sports. It's a basic tenet of money management called budgeting. All players say they do it; most players don't.

Second, I keep my bankroll and my winnings separate. In many cases, particularly if there is considerable money at issue, I'll put my winnings in a safe deposit box that most all casinos provide today. If I'm at a racetrack, I'll often ask that a big winning ticket be paid by check. For those of you who try to hide your winnings from the feds, you'll probably get a W2-G issued by the track, so what's the point? Besides, if you're going to hide your winnings, I'd rather see you hide it from crooks or from yourself! Who could do the most damage to your winnings—you, crooks, or a good tax accountant? Think about it.

2. PLAYING WITH "HOUSE MONEY"

This is a term that can only get you into trouble. The phrase is part of an old cliché among gamblers that I'm sure you've heard: "I'm betting with house money." The expression sprang up in the sportsbooks many years ago before the term "house money" was inserted for "the bookie's money." In fact, sports bettors are still the biggest victims of this charade, but I hear it around the track and in the casino too. So listen up: When the money's in your pocket, it's your money!

What difference does it make how it got there? Are your winnings a different color than your original stake? Are you applying two different values to money? I think so. And I think that this kind of attitude can only lead to reckless, senseless losses. Remember, when the money's in your pocket, it's your money! If you think of it as "house money," the house will eventually get it back. It's just another example of thinking the way the casino wants you to think.

3. ACQUIRING A SENSE OF TIMING

I don't feel that driving urge to play that most people do. I don't have an urge to play—I have an urge to win! And for me, patience almost always helps me find it. Few players catch my attention anymore, but occasionally I'll see one at a craps table who can scare the dots off the dice. There's nothing wrong with being aggressive: It's how fortunes are made. The key, of course, is timing. Aggressive players are cunning and patient. They know when to strike and they strike hard. I firmly believe that what separates winners from losers is much more than luck, and even much more than skill. It's an uncanny ability to just know when—when to jump on it, when to ease back, and when to walk.

13 WINNING MAXIMS

Winning Maxim #1

The gambler who tells everyone else how to play is always the one who wins the least.

Winning Maxim #2

Players who give worthy advice are wasting their time. Good players don't need it and fools won't heed it.

Winning Maxim #3

There are no sure things in gambling, and there are no impossible things. Everything in between is just a matter of odds.

Winning Maxim #4

You'll never win big if you don't know how to win small.

Winning Maxim #5

Most casino players think they're experts. An expert is a guy who knows 47 ways to make love, but can't find a girlfriend.

Winning Maxim #6

In the casino, you must have the ability to recognize an opportunity, the wisdom to know that you can't force it to happen, and the discipline to quit when it's gone.

Winning Maxim #7

All players love to win money; a few players just love to win.

Winning Maxim #8

Don't ever let your gambling reach the point where losing is fun, as in "We only lost a few hundred dollars, but we had fun!"

Winning Maxim #9

Believe in your instincts, not silly superstitions.

Winning Maxim #10

When you gamble, take only your most trusted friend along with you. Never gamble with a fool.

Winning Maxim #11

Having a lot of money is never a reason to bet a lot of money.

Winning Maxim #12

Winning is one thing; keeping it is another.

Winning Maxim #13

If you win and you're not excited, you haven't won at all!

Earlier in this closing chapter, I listed the three most exciting bets and topped that list with horse racing. For those of you who would argue that horse racing provides the most exciting win, I have a backup answer that perhaps is a better one:

> What is the most exciting bet you can make?
> A bet that wins!

THE CARDOZA CRAPS MASTER

Exclusive Offer! - Not Available Anywhere Else)

Three Big Strategies!

Here It is! **At last**, the **secrets** of the **Grande-Gold Power Sweep, Molliere's Monte Carlo Turnaround** and the **Montarde-D'Girard Double Reverse** - three big strategies - are made available and presented for the **first time anywhere!** These powerful strategies are designed for the serious craps player, one wishing to bring the best odds and strategies to hot tables, cold tables and choppy tables.

1. THE GRANDE-GOLD POWER SWEEP (HOT TABLE STRATEGY)

This **dynamic strategy** takes maximum advantage of hot tables and shows you how to amass small **fortunes quickly** when numbers are being thrown fast and furious. The Grande-Gold stresses aggressive betting on wagers the house has no edge on! This previously unreleased strategy will make you a powerhouse at a hot table.

2. MOLLIERE'S MONTE CARLO TURNAROUND (COLD TABLE STRATEGY)

For the player who likes betting against the dice, Molliere's Monte Carlo Turnaround shows how to turn a cold table into hot cash. Favored by an exclusive circle of professionals who will play nothing else, the uniqueness of this strongman strategy is that the vast majority of bets **give absolutely nothing away to the casino!**

3. MONTARDE-D'GIRARD DOUBLE REVERSE (CHOPPY TABLE STRATEGY)

This **new** strategy is the **latest development** and the **most exciting strategy** to be designed in recent years. **Learn how** to play the optimum strategies against the tables when the dice run hot and cold (a choppy table) with no apparent reason. **The Montarde-d'Girard Double Reverse** shows how you can **generate big profits** while less knowledgeable players are ground out by choppy dice. And, of course, the majority of our bets give nothing away to the casino!

BONUS!!! Order now, and you'll receive **The Craps Master-Professional Money Management Formula** ($15 value) **absolutely free!** Necessary for serious players and used by the pros, the Craps Master Formula features the unique **stop-loss ladder.**

The Above Offer is Not Available Anywhere Else. You Must Order Here.

To order send $75 $50 (plus postage and handling) by check or money order to:

Cardoza Publishing, P.O. Box 98115, Las Vegas, NV 89193